A New Day, New Provision

A New Day, New Provision

Volume 1

Sufi Wisdom Series

ꕤ

Shaykh Muhammad Nazim Adil

Foreword by

Shaykh Muhammad Hisham Kabbani

Published and Distributed by:

Institute for Spiritual and Cultural Advancement (ISCA)
17195 Silver Parkway, #201
Fenton, MI 48430 USA
Tel: (888) 278-6624
Fax: (810) 815-0518
Email: staff@naqshbandi.org
Web: http://www.naqshbandi.org

First Edition: August 2014
New Day, New Provision
ISBN: 978-1-938058-26-4

Library of Congress Control Number: 2014949413

Adil, Muhammad Nazim.
A New Day, New Provision/by Shaykh Muhammad Nazim Adil.
volumes cm
Includes bibliographical references.
ISBN 978-1-938058-26-4 (alk. paper)

PRINTED IN THE UNITED STATES OF AMERICA
15 14 13 12 11 05 06 07 08 09

Shaykh Muhammad Nazim Adil (1922-2014) has a remarkable lineage. He is *as-Sayyid*, a descendant of Prophet Muḥammad, (peace and blessing of God be upon him), further distinguished as *al-Hasani wal-Husayni*, a descendant of both Hasan and Husayn ibn Ali, Prophet Muhammad's grandsons. In addition, his paternal ancestry includes the illustrious 12th century saint, Shaykh Abdul-Qadir al-Jilani, founder of the Qadiri Sufi Order, and his maternal ancestry includes world-renowned 13th century poet, Jalaluddin Rumi.

Contents

Foreword

Bismillāhi 'r-Raḥmāni 'r-Raḥīm.
In the Name of God, The Most Beneficent, The Most Merciful.

All Praise is due to God, The Exalted, for the endless blessings He bestows on each of us, both what we see and know, and the infinite blessings that are unknown to us.

In these days of struggle and challenge, when people are scattered and human relationships are weak, and hearts are left searching for inner peace, through these pages we are blessed with immediate, tangible guidance which, at the very least, leads us away from the darkness of doubt and replenishes our inner strength and confidence.

This thoughtful book in the *Sufi Wisdom Series* is comprised of transcribed lectures of Shaykh Muḥammad Nazim Adil, founder of the Naqshbandiyya-Nazimiyya Sufi Order, whose timeless teachings are heavenly wisdom for all, reaching beyond ethnic, cultural, and religious barriers like illumined arrows penetrating the heart. His divinely inspired words are special gifts to one who has devoted his heart and life to The Almighty for more than seventy years.

The series as a whole presents more than two-hundred of Shaykh Nazim's lectures that cover broad topics of interest and form a unique handbook of instructions, wisdom, guidance, and support for seekers of any spiritual path.

I have been honored to follow Shaykh Nazim since my childhood in Beirut, where he often visited my family. At the tender age of ten years, Shaykh Nazim took me under his wing and later introduced me to Grandshaykh ʿAbdAllāh in Damascus, who, from our first meeting, became a grandfather figure, always loving and patient.

For more than fifty years, I witnessed Shaykh Nazim's furtherance of Grandshaykh ʿAbdAllāh's teachings and the vast audiences from around the world that gravitated to him, always seeking his healing guidance, his heartfelt advice and encouragement to serve The Almighty.

The perpetual, oft-reaching, and miraculous power of their guidance has changed individual lives, households and entire communities. I have seen countless numbers of seekers, people of all walks of life, from common citizens to heads of state, who refer to Shaykh Nazim's healing words as they navigate the challenges of daily life. Many have been healed of physical and mental illnesses; most have been blessed with a rekindled spirit.

Thus, I consider it a distinct privilege to present these teachings to you, and I pray you receive the benefit of the entire series in your spiritual journey.

Shaykh Muhammad Hisham Kabbani

Introduction

The warming late afternoon sun, subdued and filtered through the high, lead-encased panes of an old church in southeast London that now serves as a mosque, shines down upon an extraordinary group of people. It is not uncommon to see semicircles of ethnically diverse men and women of varied ages, clustered around an elderly, turbaned, white-bearded man who could have stepped straight out of the Bible or the Qur'an.

Addressing their hearts, he bathes them in a sublimely eloquent discourse in his distinctive style, punctuated by many savory examples and endless humor about the necessity of a seeker emptying his heart of everything except God.

A newcomer to the group is likely to feel both awe and love for the possessor of that luminous face with its large, expressive blue eyes. They are touched by his speech and warmed by the graciousness of his welcome. And to his millions of followers now spread throughout the world, this simple, humble, but supremely luminous, saintly man is the most revered and loved of all people on Earth. He is their teacher, counselor, guide, and living example of the Islamic faith in its fullest embodiment, their beloved "Shaykh Nazim."

As founder and *murshid* (spiritual guide) of the Naqshbandiyya Nazimiyya Sufi Order, Shaykh Nazim is an inheritor of fifteen centuries of the highest Islamic knowledge of both the external and spiritual sciences. Although he is a man of the East, he speaks to Western followers in his inimitable brand of English that reaches the heart and punctuates his talks with unfailing humor and moving anecdotes.

Since the dawn of humanity, God Most High has revealed His guidance to Mankind through His prophets and messengers, including Noah, Abraham, Ishmael, Isaac, Jacob, Joseph, Lot, Moses, David, Solomon, and Jesus, peace be upon them all. A descendant of Abraham, namely Muḥammad ﷺ, the Seal of Prophets, brought the final revelation from God to all Mankind, but although there are no longer prophets on Earth, the Most Merciful Lord has not left His servants without inspired teachers and guides. *Awlīyā*, holy souls or saints, are the Inheritors of the prophets. Up to the Last Day, these "friends of God," beacons of truth, righteousness and the highest spirituality, will continue in the footsteps of the prophets, calling people to their Lord and guiding seekers to His glorious Divine Presence.

One such inspired teacher, a shaykh or *murshid* of the Naqshbandiyya Nazimiyya Sufi Order, is Shaykh Nazim Adil. A descendant not only of the Holy Prophet Muḥammad ﷺ, but also of the great Sufi masters ʿAbdul Qadir al-Jilani and Jalaluddin Rumi, Shaykh Nazim was born in 1922 in Larnaca, Cyprus during British rule of the island. Gifted from earliest childhood with an extraordinary spiritual personality, young Nazim received his spiritual training in Damascus over forty years at the hands of the eminent shaykh ʿAbdAllāh ad-Daghestani, fondly referred to as "Grandshaykh", mentor of well-known figures Gurjieff[1] and J. G. Bennett[2]. Before leaving this life in 1973, Grandshaykh designated Shaykh Nazim as his successor.

In 1974, Shaykh Nazim went to London for the first time, initiating his well-known annual Ramadan visit that continued into the late 1990s. A small circle of followers began to grow around him, eagerly taking their training in the ways of Islam and *Ṭarīqat* (the spiritual path). From this humble beginning, the circle has grown to include millions of *murīds* (disciples) in various countries of the world that includes illustrious individuals, both religious and secular.

Shaykh Nazim's luminous, spiritual personality radiates love, compassion and goodness, and he is regarded by many of his *murīds* as the Sulṭān al-Awlīyā (King of Saints) of this time.

---

[1] G. I. Gurdjieff (1866-1949) was an influential spiritual teacher of the early to mid-20th century who taught that most humans live in a state of hypnotic "waking sleep", but it is possible to transcend to a higher state of consciousness and achieve full human potential through his discipline "The Work" (work on oneself) or "The Method".

[2] John G. Bennett was a trusted Gurjieff disciple who helped spread the latter's teachings. In 1953, he undertook a long journey to the Middle East and initially met Shaykh `AbdAllāh ad-Daghestani, whom he described as "a true saint in whom one feels an immediate, complete trust. With him there were no lengthy arguments or quotations from the scriptures." Their meeting on Mt. Qasiyoun in Damascus is narrated in Bennett's book *Subud,* in which he concludes the shaykh was in possession of, "powers of a kind that…prepared me to take very seriously anything he might say."

The shaykh reaches through a subtle interweaving of personal example and talks ("associations" or *ṣuḥbahs*), invariably delivered extempore according to the inspirations he receives. He does not lecture, but rather pours from his heart into hearts of his listeners knowledge and wisdoms that may change their innermost beings and bring them toward their Lord as His humble, willing, loving servants.

Shaykh Nazim's language and style are so poignant that not only do his teachings seem inspired, but also his extraordinary use of words. His *ṣuḥbahs* represent the teachings of a Twentieth century Sufi master, firmly grounded in Islamic orthodoxy. He speaks sincerely and directly to hearts of seekers of God of any faith, in a tremendous outpouring of truth, wisdom and divine knowledge that is surely unparalleled in the English language, guiding the seeker toward the Divine Presence. The sum total of his message is that of hope, love, mercy, and reassurance.

In a troubled and uncertain world in which old, time-honored values have given place to new ones of confused origins and unclear prospects, in which a feeling heart and thinking mind is constantly troubled by a sense of things being terribly disordered and out of control, in which the future seems forebodingly dark and uncertain for humanity, he proclaims God's love and care for His servants, and invites them to give their hearts to Him.

Shaykh Nazim holds out to seekers the assurance that even their smallest steps toward their Lord will not go unnoticed, nor neglected. Rather than threatening sinners with the prospect of eternal Hell, he offers hope of salvation from the Most Merciful Lord, and heart-warming encouragement and incentive for inner change and growth. As one who has traversed every step of the seeker's path and reached its pinnacle, he offers both inner and practical guidelines for attaining the highest spiritual goals.

All the books in this series are based on talks given extempore, as Shaykh Nazim never prepares his words, but invariably speaks according to inspirations coming to his heart.

In keeping with the shaykh's methodology—of the prophets, particularly of the Last Prophet, Muḥammad—of reinforcing vital lessons by repetition and reiteration, the same themes and anecdotes recur again and again. The talks seem to come in unannounced clusters, centered on a primary theme that develops and evolves according to the spiritual state of the listeners. Thus, Shaykh Nazim may cite the same verse or a *Ḥadīth* (Holy Tradition), or tell the same tale on different occasions, each time reinforcing a slightly different aspect of the eternal message of love and light, which is embodied in the Islamic faith.

Shaykh Nazim was fluent in Arabic, Turkish, Greek, and 'the King's English'. Over five decades, his lectures have been translated into twenty or more languages that, to date, have reached the most remote areas of the world. His talks are interspersed with words and phrases from Arabic and other Islamic languages that are translated either in the text itself or in a footnote the first time they occur.

Every attempt has been made to retain the shaykh's original language with minimal editing. However, some inadvertent errors may have found their way into the text and for these, we ask Allāh's forgiveness and your kind indulgence. May your heart be filled with light and love as you read and reflect upon these inspired words.

Publisher's Notes

As some terms may be foreign, transliterations are provided, as well as a brief glossary. Quotes from the Holy Qur'ān and Holy Traditions of Prophet Muḥammad are offset, italicized, and cited.

The pronoun "they" is frequently used by Sufi guides to reference heavenly beings and holy souls who support them and give them orders, a usage that appears throughout this book.

Where gender-specific pronouns such as "he" and "him" are applied in a general sense, no discrimination is intended towards women, upon whom The Almighty bestowed great honor.

Muslims typically offer salutations upon speaking, hearing or reading the name of Prophet Muḥammad and other prophets, his family, his companions, and saints. We have applied the following international standard:

﷾ *Subḥānahu wa Ta*ʿalā (may His Glory be Exalted), following the name "Allāh" and any of the Islamic names of God.

ﷺ *ṢallAllāhu ʿalayhi wa sallam* (God's blessings and greetings of peace be upon him), following the names of Prophet Muḥammad.

عليه السلام *ʿAlayhi (ʿalayha) ʿs-salām* (peace be upon him/her) following names of other prophets, names of Prophet Muḥammad's relatives, the pure and virtuous women in Islam, and angels.

رضي الله عنها/رضي الله عنه *Raḍī*Allāhu *ʿanh(um)* (may God be pleased with him/her), following names of Companions of Prophet Muḥammad; plural: *raḍī*Allāhu *ʿanhum.*

ق *Qaddas*Allāhu *sirrah* (may God sanctify his secret) following names of saints.

Transliteration

To facilitate authentic pronunciation of names, places and terms, use the following key:

Symbol	Transliteration	Symbol	Transliteration	Vowels: Long	
ء	’	ط	ṭ	آ ى	ā
ب	b	ظ	ẓ	و	ū
ت	t	ع	‘	ي	ī
ث	th	غ	gh	Short	
ج	j	ف	f		a
ح	ḥ	ق	q		u
خ	kh	ك	k		i
د	d	ل	l		
ذ	dh	م	m		
ر	r	ن	n		
ز	z	ه	h		
س	s	و	w		
ش	sh	ي	y		
ص	ṣ	ة	ah; at		
ض	ḍ	ال	al-/’l-		

Masters of the Naqshbandi Golden Chain

We believe mentioning the names of these holy souls brings peace.
May Allāh ﷻ preserve their secrets.

1. Prophet Muḥammad ibn ʿAbdAllāh ﷺ
2. Abū Bakr aṣ-Ṣiddīq
3. Salmān al-Fārsī
4. Qāsim bin Muḥammad bin Abū Bakr
5. Jaʿfar aṣ-Ṣādiq
6. Ṭayfūr Abū Yazīd al-Bistāmī
7. Abūl-Ḥassan ʿAlī al-Kharqānī
8. Abū ʿAlī al-Farmadī
9. Abū Yaʿqūb Yūsuf al-Ḥamadānī
10. Abūl-ʿAbbās, al-Khiḍr
11. ʿAbdul-Khāliq al-Ghujdawānī
12. ʿArif ar-Riwakrī
13. Khwāja Maḥmūd al-Anjīr al-Faghnawī
14. ʿAlī ar-Ramitānī
15. Muḥammad Bābā as-Samāsī
16. As-Sayyid Amīr Kulāl
17. Muḥammad Bahāuddīn Shāh Naqshband
18. ʿAlāuddīn al-Bukhārī al-ʿAṭṭār
19. Yaʿqūb al-Charkhī
20. ʿUbaydullāh al-Ahrār
21. Muḥammad az-Zāhid
22. Darwish Muḥammad
23. Muḥammad Khwāja al-Amkanakī
24. Muḥammad al-Bāqī bilLāh
25. Aḥmad al-Farūqī as-Sirhindī
26. Muḥammad al-Maʿṣūm
27. Muḥammad Sayfuddīn al-Fārūqī al-Mujaddidī
28. As-Sayyid Nūr Muḥammad al-Badawānī
29. Shamsuddīn Ḥabīb Allāh
30. ʿAbdAllāh ad-Dahlawī
31. Khālid al-Baghdādī
32. Ismāʿīl Muḥammad ash-Shirwānī
33. Khāṣ Muḥammad Shirwānī
34. Muḥammad Effendī al-Yarāghī
35. Jamāluddīn al-Ghumūqī al-Ḥusaynī
36. Abū Aḥmad aṣ-Ṣughūrī
37. Abū Muḥammad al-Madanī
38. Sharafuddīn ad-Dāghestānī
39. ʿAbdAllāh al-Fāʾiz ad-Dāghestānī
40. Muḥammad Nāẓim ʿAdil

40th Sufi Master of the Eminent Naqshbandi Golden Chain

As-Sayyid Shaykh Muḥammad Nazim Adil an-Naqshbandī

He is the Imam of the People of Sincerity, the Secret of Sainthood, who revived the Naqshbandi Order at the end of the 20th Century with Heavenly guidance and Prophetic ethics. He infused into the Nation and the Planet the love of God and love of the Lovers of God after they had been darkened with the fire and smoke of tribulation and terror, anger and grief!

He is the Unveiler of Secrets, the Keeper of Light, the Shaykh of Shaykhs, the Sultan of Ascetics, the Sultan of the Pious, the Sultan of the People of the Truth. He is the Chief Master without peer of the Divine Knowledge in the late 20th Century. He is the Rain from the Ocean of Knowledge of this Order, which is reviving spirits in all parts of this world. He is the Saint of the Seven Continents, his light having attracted disciples and students from all quarters of the globe. He wears the Cloak of the Light of the Divine Presence. He is unique in his time. He is the orchid planted in the earth of Divine Love. He is the Sun for all the universes. He is known as the Saint of the Two Wings: the external knowledge and the internal knowledge!

He is a Miracle of Allāh's Miracles, walking on the Earth and soaring in the Heavens. He is a Secret of Allāh's Secrets, appearing in His Divinity and Existing in His Existence. He is the Owner of the Throne of Guidance, the Reviver of Divine Law, the Master of Sufi Way, the Builder of the Truth, the Guide of the Circle, the Lyric Poem of All the Secrets! He is the Master of Saints and the Saint of the Masters! Seekers circle the Kaʿbah of His Light.

He is a fountain always flowing, a waterfall continuously cascading, a river always flooding, an ocean endlessly cresting and breaking on infinite shores!

His Noble Station

As Shah Naqshband was the *Mujaddid* in Bukhara and Central Asia, as Sayyidina Ahmad as-Sirhindī al-Mujaddedi was the Reviver of the 2nd Millennium, as Sayyidina Khalid al-Baghdadi was the Reviver of Islam and Shari'ah and *Ṭarīqat* in the Middle East, Shaykh Muhammad Nazim Adil an-Naqshbandi is the Reviver, the Renewer and the Caller to God in this Age of Technology and Material Progress!

A Glimpse of the Legendary Life of Mawlana Shaykh Nazim

Shaykh Muḥammad Nazim Adil was born in 1922 in Larnaca, Cyprus into an aristocratic family deeply rooted in Ottoman culture. His paternal lineage is traced to Sayyīdinā ʿAbdul Qadir al-Jilani, founder of the Qadiri Sufi Order. His maternal lineage is traced to Sayyīdinā Jalaluddin Rumi, founder of the Mevlevi Sufi Order. Mawlana Shaykh Nazim is Hasani-Husayni, directly related to the Prophet (s) through his noble grandfathers to the Family of the Prophet (s) From his father's side he received the Qadiri Ṭarīqat and from his mother's side, the Mevlevi Ṭarīqat.

Childhood and Early Religious Training

During his childhood in Cyprus, Shaykh Nazim was given great consideration because of his unusually high spiritual station. Everyone in Larnaca knew about him, because at a young age he was able to advise people and reveal their future spontaneously. From age five, there were times he went missing, and his mother often found him either in the mosque or at the grave of Umm ul-Hiram (r), a Companion of the Prophet (s). He also sat with his grandfather, a Qadiri shaykh, to learn its discipline and spirituality. Extraordinary signs appeared early in him. His conduct was perfect: he never fought nor argued with anyone and he was always smiling and patient.

His father sent him to school to study secular knowledge during the day and in the evening he studied the religious sciences. His paternal and maternal grandfathers trained him for the spiritual path. He was a genius among his fellow students. After completing high school, every night he studied the Mevlevi and Qadiri Ṭarīqats, and soon he conducted their *dhikr* circles on Thursdays and Fridays.

Higher Education and First Shaykh

In 1940, he attended University of Istanbul, where he and his siblings pursued higher education. He received a degree in Chemistry, a passion that later disinterested him when he could not save his older brother from dying. Thereafter, he became deeply immersed in the study of traditional Islam and *Taṣawwuf,* Sufism was eventually led to the spiritual guide he had beheld in dreams.

During his first year in Istanbul, he met his first spiritual guide, Shaykh Sulayman Arzarumi[3] (d. 1948), from whom he learned the discipline of the Naqshbandi Order, in addition to the Qadiri and Mevlevi Orders. He was often seen in Sultan Ahmad's Mosque, meditating by himself throughout the night.

In 1943, Shaykh Sulayman sent the young disciple on a journey of test and trials to reach his true shaykh, Sulṭān al-Awlīyā ʿAbdAllāh al-Fa'iz ad-Daghestani of Damascus (d. 1973), 39th Master of the esteemed Naqshbandi Golden Chain that originates with Prophet Muḥammad, may the peace and blessing of God be upon him. Finally, 18 months later, he took bayaʿ with Shaykh ʿAbdAllāh, spent the night with him in Damascus, experienced great miracles, and was sent to Cyprus the following day!

Cyprus

Due to the regional military fighting of WWI, the trip to Cyprus was not only dangerous, but nearly impossible. About this, Shaykh Nazim said:

> As soon as I landed and put my foot on Cyprus soil, immediately a spiritual vision was opened to my heart. I saw Grandshaykh ʿAbdAllāh ad-Daghestani saying to me, "O my son. Nothing was able to keep you from carrying out my order. You have achieved a lot by listening and accepting. From this moment, I will always be visible to you. Anytime you direct your heart towards me, I will be there. Any question you have, you will receive an answer directly from the Divine Presence. Any spiritual state you wish to achieve, it will be granted to you because of your complete submission. The Saints are all happy with you, the Prophet (s) is happy with you." As soon as he said that, I felt

[3] One of the 313 saints of the Naqshbandi Order, who represent the 313 messengers.

him beside me and since then he has never left me, he is always beside me.

In Cyprus, his first task was to call *adhān* in Arabic from minaret of the local mosque, which was then illegal. He was jailed a week, released, and continued to defy the law, walking from town to town, climbing the minaret of every local mosque, and calling the *adhān* in Arabic. In total, the government brought 114 lawsuits against him, which could have resulted in 110 years in prison, but Shaykh Nazim was undeterred. The day of the court hearing, Adnan Menderes was elected[4], and his first act was to repeal the ban on the public call of *adhān* in Arabic! This was a miracle.

During these years in Cyprus, Shaykh Nazim traveled the entire country, as well Lebanon, Egypt, Saudi Arabia and other places to teach the Ṭarīqat. He moved back to Damascus in 1952, when he got married to one of the murids of Grandshaykh, Hajjah Amina Adil. From that time he lived in Damascus, and every year he would visit Cyprus for the three months of Rajab, Shaʿban and Ramadan. His family lived in Damascus with him and would travel with him to Cyprus when he went there. He had two daughters and two sons.

Marriage, Family, Seclusions, Hajj and Travels

In 1952, Shaykh Nazim returned to Damascus, where Grandshaykh ʿAbdAllāh married him to another disciple who was like a daughter, Hajjah Amina.

Years before, her faithful family had fled religious persecution in Communist Russia and settled in Turkey, then later in Damascus. Shaykh Nazim and Hajjah Amina began married life near Grandshaykh ʿAbdAllāh's place on Jabal Qasiyoun, a famous area of Damascus, and later raised their growing family between Damascus and Cyprus, where he returned annually for the holy month Rajab, Shaʿban and Ramadan. In Damascus, their modest stucco home was never empty of visitors. They often hosted 100 visitors daily, whom Shaykh Nazim personally served.

---

[4] Turkish Prime Minister, 1950–1960

Shaykh Nazim was ordered by Grandshaykh ʿAbdAllāh into seclusion (*khalwah*) several times, six months, a year or more, where he trained in advanced Sufi Sciences and was disciplined in the ways of self-denial.

Grandshaykh sent him annually as Hajj leader of Cypriot *murid* pilgrims, a serious trust thought which he attended to their needs and led them through all the rites of Hajj. Shaykh Nazim completed 27 pilgrimages in total.

He was also known for his grassroots walking tours from village to village throughout Turkey and Cyprus. He walked one or two days, reached a village, spent a week teaching the Naqshbandi Way, led dhikr, trained the people, then continued to the next village. Soon his name was on every tongue, from the border of Jordan to the border of Turkey near Aleppo, and throughout Cyprus, where he became so beloved that the dark green color of his turban was uniquely known as his color.

Grandshaykh's Predictions, Establishing a Base in London

In 1973, before Grandshaykh ʿAbdAllāh passed away, he appointed Shaykh Nazim as his spiritual heir and successor, whereupon Shaykh Nazim assumed the title Sulṭān al-Awlīyā, 40th Master of the Naqshbandi Golden Chain.

In his will, Grandshaykh ʿAbdAllāh predicted Shaykh Nazim would open Naqshbandi centers in the United Kingdom and bring traditional Islam to Europe. Fulfilling the order of his shaykh, Shaykh Nazim traveled to London in 1974 without knowing a soul there or relying on anyone. Within a few short years, he established a broad following of native Muslims and converts from throughout the UK and Europe.

As a global melting pot, London was the perfect backdrop to reach people from around the world. In the late 1970s and throughout the 1980's, Shaykh Nazim traveled the Middle East, Europe, Southeast Asia, and Far East.. By 1980, three large mosques and a major Naqshbandi center at St. Anne's served as the growing multi-cultural group's western base in London, while Cyprus remained its eastern base.

Expansion to North America

In 1991, Shaykh Nazim sent his son-in-law, Shaykh Hisham Kabbani, to represent him in the United States. By 1995, Shaykh Hisham had established fifteen Naqshbandi centers throughout the U.S. and Canada that attracted thousands of native Muslims and converts. Promoting the teachings of the Naqshbandi Sufi Masters, the new centers offered a peaceful, tolerant, loving alternative to the growing Islamist rhetoric that then permeated mosques and Islamic centers. To date, under Shaykh Hisham's direction the number of Naqshbandi centers in the U.S. and Canada has tripled.

Shaykh Nazim visited his growing North America flock regularly throughout the 1990s and early 2000s. At the urging of Shaykh Hisham, he was keynote speaker at the prestigious International Islamic Unity Conferences (IIUC).

In 1996, at IIUC-I in Los Angeles, he urged 150 globally renowned Islamic scholars to unite in bringing their followers back to moderate Islamic teachings and the Holy Traditions of Prophet Muḥammad ﷺ, with the goal of establishing peace and eliminating ignorance. There, Shaykh Nazim also proclaimed "The Day of the Orphan" and led a peaceful march through downtown Los Angeles that was praised by local and national media outlets, with video clips of the event featured on nightly news.

In 1998, his inaugural address at IIUC-II in Washington DC was a harsh condemnation of terrorism, in light of that day's horrific bombings of U.S. Embassies in Dar es-Salām and Nairobi. Shaykh Nazim was the first and most vociferous Muslim leader to condemn the bombings as a categorical violation of Islamic teachings. The speech was broadcast live on C-SPAN and featured on CNN, BBC, BBC America, Voice of America and Fox News. Reuters and the Associated Press (AP) issued press releases of the speech that were published in major newspapers around the world.

Always Spoke Truth to Power

Throughout his illustrious life, Shaykh Nazim had no trouble speaking truth to power, always pointing to divine orders and obligations. During that visit to Washington DC, by invitation, Shaykh Nazim addressed the prestigious

National Press Club regarding the rise of global terrorism and what must be done to eliminate it.

He also addressed U.S. Congress about the oppression of Muslims in Bosnia and Kosovo, and introduced a contingent of Balkan Muslim scholars attending IIUC-II at Shaykh Nazim's invitation, who spoke of their tragic on-the-ground experiences. This effort is known to have positively influenced the outcome of the Kosovo War.

In September 2000, Shaykh Nazim addressed the United Nations in New York as keynote speaker at the World Conference on Religion and Peace (WCRP), a global organization of which he and Shaykh Hisham were advisory members. There, before thousands of religious leaders, he extolled Mankind's duty to their Lord by respecting His Creation, fighting oppression, and caring for refugees and the downtrodden. When Shaykh Nazim openly led the Islamic prayer in the U.N., despite being swiftly told by officials it was not allowed, he continued and said, "It is only with Allāh Almighty's help that people will be served, so we call on Him."

2001 Historic World Tour

At Shaykh Nazim's direction, Shaykh Hisham arranged a world tour from April-July 2001, starting with an historic three-week tour of holy sites in Uzbekistan as guests of the president. The contingent of 150 Naqshbandis was warmly received by government officials and religious leaders in Tashkent, Samarkand and Bukhara.

Afterwards, Shaykh Nazim continued his world tour to South Africa, Malaysia, Indonesia, Singapore, Japan, Sri Lanka, and Pakistan, where he met with top government officials, industrialists, celebrities, religious leaders and common folk who sought his blessing and spiritual guidance of how to better serve Allāh Almighty and bring peace in their hearts.

Due to aging and a decline in health, after many long years of divine service, it was his final trip abroad and thereafter he remained in Lefke, Cyprus, where his followers visited.

Launch of Sufilive Daily Broadcast

In 2009, to bridge the geographical distance between Shaykh Nazim and his followers, Shaykh Hisham introduced a live, one-hour English broadcast with the aging shaykh from Cyprus on Sufilive.com[5]. Thousands of viewers around the world tuned in daily to hear the teachings of the Naqshbandi Sufi Masters and divine inspirations, which again breathed life into Shaykh Nazim's universal message to love Allāh Almighty, serve and respect His Creation, remain vigilant against those who deny Him, and to support good and avoid evil.

His Teachings Reach around the World

Since the 1970s, every year tens of thousands of faithful visited Mawlana Shaykh Nazim at his home and mosque in Cyprus to seek his blessing, spiritual protection, and heavenly intercession. His millions of followers include royalty, heads of state, high-level politicians, celebrities, industrialists, religious leaders, and common folk.

Books, Videos and Influence on Pop Culture

More than 200 books of his teachings have been printed in English, Turkish, Arabic, French, Spanish, Malay and other major languages. More than 1800 videos of his talks are archived for public viewing on Sufilive.com. An Internet search of his name brings 60,000 hits. Hundreds of websites in multiple languages are devoted to his teachings. Through his unceasing outreach, millions all over the world have embraced Islam.

In addition, it is well documented that the Star Wars series is rooted not only in *Taṣawwuf*, but specifically in teachings of Mawlana Shaykh Nazim. In 1975-76, film producer George Lucas spent time with Naqshbandis in Northern California and the UK while developing his original script and characters.

---

[5] Those historic discourses, along with thousands of others, can be viewed and downloaded for free in the Sufilive.com video archive.

In April 2014, after more than a year of declining health, Shaykh Muḥammad Nazim Adil was rushed to hospital, where he was treated for heart failure. Thousands of well-wishers flocked to Cyprus to pray for his recovery. Sadly, on 7 May, Shaykh Nazim passed from this world. His funeral was broadcast live in Turkey, Pakistan, by Ummah Channel in the UK, and on the Internet. News of his passing was featured around the world by both major and small broadcast and print media outlets.

Miracles of his passing and burial are included in this book that hopefully will bring you, dear reader, to our beloved Sulṭān al-Awlīyā, Mawlana Shaykh Nazim Adil's illumined presence. May your burdens be lifted and your heart filled with love, peace, happiness and spiritual devotion from his sacred, uplifting words! *Amīn.*

In Memoriam

Bismillāhi 'r-Raḥmāni 'r-Raḥīm.
In the Name of God, The Most Beneficent, The Most Merciful.

It is with hearts burning with grief and eyes filled with tears that we state that after a difficult illness, our Master, our Teacher, our Saint, our Guide, *Sulṭān al-Awlīyā* Mawlana Shaykh Muḥammad Nazim Adil ق, has passed from this worldly life today and moved to *al-Rafiq al-ʿAlā*, the Highest Companionship of Allāh *ʿAzza wa Jall* and His Beloved Prophet, Sayyīdinā Muḥammad ﷺ.

He was the majestic and noble leader of millions of people around the world who will feel a great void in their temporal lives without his physical presence to comfort them.

We will observe three days of mourning on Mawlana's behalf. We request all Mawlana Shaykh's *murīds* around the world to pray *Janaza Ghayb* for Mawlana, to recite *Surah YaSin, Sūrat al-Mulk, Tahlīl, Salawāt, Khatm Khawajagan* and to serve meals in the name of Mawlana Shaykh Nazim, gifting the reward for his soul.

Visiting Mawlana Shaykh ق in his grave has an importance and a great meaning.

مَنْ زَارَ قَبْرِي وَجَبَتْ لَهُ شَفَاعَتِي

The Prophet ﷺ said: Whoever visits my grave, my intercession will be guaranteed for him.[6]

[6] Ibn `Umar by al-Bayhaqi, al-Hakeem at-Tirmidhi, ad-Daraqutnee, al-Bazzār, ibn Khuzaymah and others.

Awlīyāullāh, the friends of Allāh, are inheritors of the Prophet ﷺ, and if someone visits them they will intercede in the holy presence of the Prophet ﷺ for that person. For this, we must all be happy!

Those who came from all around the world and those who had intention to come but were not able will be under that message, *inshā'Allāh*, that our *shuyūkh* will intercede in front of Prophet ﷺ, for all of us to be accepted by Prophet ﷺ!

Wa 's-salāmu ʿalaykum wa raḥmatullāhi wa barakātuh.[7]

Shaykh Muḥammad Hisham Kabbani
8 Rajab 1435 / 7 May 2014
Lefke, Cyprus

ꟾ

[7] And peace be with you, and Allāh's mercy and blessings.

Extraordinary Miracles of Mawlana Shaykh Nazim's Passing

بسۡمِ ٱللهِ ٱلرَّحۡمَـٰنِ ٱلرَّحِيمِ

Inna lillāhi wa inna ilayhi raji'ūn.

As-salām 'alaykum wa raḥmatullāhi wa barakātuh.

Inna alladhīna amanū wa 'āmilū 's-sālihāti kānat lahum jannātu 'l-firdawsi nuzulan, khalidīna fihā lā yabghawna 'anhā hiwalla.

Dear lovers, followers, *murīds,* disciples of Sulṭān al-Awlīyā, Mawlana Shaykh Muḥammad Nazim Adil ق. As Prophet ﷺ said in an authentic *Ḥadīth, idhkurū mahāsin mawtākum,* "Mention the good tidings of your deceased." So we wanted to share with you the miracles Mawlana Shaykh Nazim showed us after his passing.

How the Holy Soul was Taken

When the doctors assembled to decide on removing the respirator, the decision was not left in their hands; rather, Allāh ﷻ showed His love to His sincere *wali* by gently taking his soul before the doctors could attempt to assert their will. There was no medical explanation for why Mawlana Shaykh's heart stopped and his soul left his physical body before the breathing tube was removed. This was an unprecedented event, never before seen by either doctor during their long medical careers. In this way, Allāh's Will was shown to reign above that of modern medicine and that Allāh ﷻ took Mawlana to His Divine Presence and the Presence of the Prophet ﷺ when He willed.

Rain in May

In Cyprus and throughout the Middle East, the last time it rained in May was 42 years ago, yet the day of Mawlana's passing, there was powerful thunder and flashes of lightning that awoke people from their sleep. It rained heavily non-stop for two days. After two or three days of big waves, the ocean became suddenly calm. Even in Mecca and Madinah, rain fell at the time Mawlana's soul left his body. Later that afternoon, everyone realized even the sky was weeping for the loss of the world's great saint. The rain was a mercy from Allāh to show how much love He has for His saint.

Airline Seating Allocated to His Followers

Despite numerous daily flights scheduled to land in Cyprus from all over the world, all flights were overbooked and there were no seats available due to the great demand of Mawlana Shaykh's students (given priority seating) who came from around the world to pay their respects.

Mawlana's Physical Length Increased in the Grave

Many people witnessed an amazing incident during the burial of Mawlana Shaykh in his *masjid* in Lefke. Men had dug a very large grave approximately four meters [13 feet] in length. Four people stood in the grave to place Mawlana Shaykh's holy body inside. As they carried his beloved body down into the grave it was weightless, like a feather. When they laid his holy body down, miraculously it became long enough to fill the grave from one end to the other: his head touched one end and his feet touched the other. To turn his head towards *Qiblah,* we had to dig a little bit in order to accommodate his blessed head, because he was so long!

Mawlana was showing us that for *Awlīyāullāh,* even if the grave is this big Allāh makes it huge, even if it is this small Allāh makes it huge, because Allāh turns the grave of a *mu'min,* especially of a *wali,* into a piece of Paradise. We ask Allāh to turn our graves into a piece of Paradise, because either it will be a piece of Paradise or it will be a piece of Hellfire, so may Allāh protect us! This was to show all present that Mawlana was inheriting from the Prophetic Tradition of being a stature and size exceeding normal human beings.

Never during a burial has anyone seen a body stretch until the grave is almost insufficient. Perhaps if we were to increase Mawlana's grave to ten meters, Mawlana's body might stretch to fill it! That was a tremendous indication that he truly is the Inheritor of Prophet Muḥammad ﷺ!

Media Tributes

Mawlana Shaykh Nazim had earned the love and respect of so many world leaders, royal families, and great personalities that his home and *masjid* were filled with esteemed dignitaries. We received condolences from all around the world, from prime ministers, foreign ministers, big scholars and the news media, all praising him. Many news outlets around the world covered Mawlana Shaykh's burial live and spoke about his great life of promoting religious pluralism and respect, condemning terrorism and extremism, and extending his hand to members of every faith. They recalled his historical embrace of Pope Benedict XVI in Cyprus in 2010. This is an important sign that Allāh honored him both in *dunyā* and in *Akhirah*. This is for a *mu'min*: Allāh makes everyone love him and speak about him, while someone who is not a *mu'min*, Allāh doesn't care for him. May Allāh ﷻ make us *mu'min*!

During his life, Mawlana Shaykh Nazim appeared many times on TV all around the world. From his childhood, his way was to encourage open communication and friendly relations with everyone, even those who differ in opinion. He always sought cooperation with others to benefit humanity and to create a more peaceful world. Before he left this temporal world, he planted in the hearts of his followers and in the hearts of countless human beings the love and compassion for which he was so famous, so they could carry his legacy forward.

Mawlana Shaykh Nazim established countless centers in nearly every nation of the world, in which they teach mindfulness, chanting therapy and other educational programs that promote peace, love and happiness. He rejected all forms of extremism and radicalism, and embodied the Prophet's ﷺ teaching, "We Muslims are a moderate Nation".

Today is *dhikr* day, the first Thursday after the burial. Please take this opportunity to share these incidents and other memories you have of our beloved shaykh with others, especially with those who may not have had the pleasure of knowing him.

It is also important to remember when you are making *du¿a* and *dhikr*, make sure to connect your heart to those whom you love: Allāh ﷻ, His Prophet ﷺ, His *Awlīyā*. Don't listen to gossip or to people causing confusion, but keep your focus on the beloved ones and remember them.

On behalf of Sufilive, the Islamic Supreme Council of America, and our many affiliated organizations around the world, we encourage everyone to follow in Mawlana Shaykh Nazim's footsteps and implement his teachings of love, peace, acceptance and the brotherhood of humanity.

Shaykh Muḥammad Hisham Kabbani

15 May 2014

New Day, New Provision

As-salāmu ʿalaykum, yā hādirūn. Salām on those who are present. *Salām* or peace descends from the Heavens; may we also be granted from that *salām* Allāh Almighty greets His servants with, *"Salām." Allāhu Akbar! Allāhu Akbar wa lillāhi 'l-ḥamd*! *Shukr* to our Lord, *Allāhu Akbar!*

Today is *Rabīʿ 'l-Awwal,* the month of the birth of our Prophet ﷺ, the night of his holy birth. We celebrated it and then joy, glad tidings and power came to us. There is no one who opens his hands or goes to the door of the Sulṭān and returns empty-handed. O Lord, may this ignorance leave us! It has become the time when ignorance covers the world; if you ask, they don't know faith. We ask for Your help and guidance, which will save us from ignorance, for the honor of Your Beloved One ﷺ. We ask and expect this from the Beloved ﷺ. Our Umm Hiram Sulṭān also sends us support. May the honor of the honorable Companions ؓ increase more and more.

As-salāmu ʿalaykum[8]*, ayyuha 'l-hādirūn,* those who are present, *salāms* to you! *Dastūr, yā RijālAllāh*[9]! O *Mukhlisīn*, sincere servants of Allāh, those who love Allāh, the holy ones who live on the way of Allāh's love! We ask for your support. May you send us support.

We may also begin by saying, *"Aʿūdhu billāhi min ash-Shayṭāni 'r-rajīm*[10]*. Bismillāhi 'r-Raḥmāni 'r-Raḥīm."* Our way is the way of *ṣuḥbah.* What is *ṣuḥbah*? *Ṣuḥbah* is the assembly which injects every person with the strength he needs. When you run out of gas in your car, you go to a gas station, you fill up your car at the station and go on driving. The secret is in that station: it fills up something, but when it runs out you are finished and left stranded. You start searching for gas, saying, "My car ran out of gas and it is of no use now." With each *ṣuḥbah*, a new power is granted to our spirituality.

Our physical being will perish and become earth, but our reality does not die. Our physical being will die; it will be buried and will become earth. They say, "It came from earth and returns to earth." Therefore, every day

---

[8] "Peace be with you", the Muslim greeting exhorted in the Holy Qur'ān.

[9] "Give us permission, O Men of God; (I seek your help)."

[10] "I seek refuge in Allāh from the accursed Shayṭān!"

there is a new provision, *Yawmun jadīd, rizqun jadīd,* meaning, "New day, new provision." *Yawmun jadīd, rizqun jadīd. Rizq* is the material provision for our physical being and there is also a spiritual provision for our spirituality. Therefore, Man seeks provision for his exterior body and also for his spirituality, which keeps us alive; it does not crush us and does not let us be crushed. Our spirituality is a dragon!

"Our sermon is *ṣuḥbah,*" said the great ones, and I am a weak servant who is ordered to collect and arrange the few words that they granted us and to present them to the Children of Adam ﷺ. Huge planes fly in the sky when they take the power they need; how astonishing! It is also given to us to make a short *ṣuḥbah* here for whoever is present, whether it is one person, two people or more; whoever is present here may listen. I don't know anything, but they are making me speak. If there are donkeys in the assembly, give them barley; if they are human, give them food; if someone is a great person, give something accordingly.

Provision is of two kinds: one for our physical being and one for our spirituality. One whose animal side dominates constantly looks for food for his physical being, for his stomach. One whose spirituality is strong seeks from the Heavens and wants to rise to the Heavens. *SubḥānAllāh!*

O believer, listen! Our words are a few, but scattered; really we are saying them in order to present the *Bismillāh,* a "preface" so we could start the *ṣuḥbah* and tell about its importance.

What is the heading or preface of our *ṣuḥbah*? "*Bismillāhi 'r-Raḥmāni 'r-Raḥīm.*" Stand up! You are a lion! The one who says the *Bismillāh* is a lion and the one who doesn't say it is fertilizer! Therefore, we said, "*Bismillāhi 'r-Raḥmāni 'r-Raḥīm.*" How beautiful, how sweet, what an endless treasure! *Allāhu Akbar! Allāhu Akbar!*

وَإِنَّ جُندَنَا لَهُمُ الْغَالِبُونَ

And that verily Our hosts would [in the end] be victorious![11]

Say, "*Bismillāhi 'r-Raḥmāni 'r-Raḥīm*" and don't fear! Now a lot of new, imitated weapons have come out. *Allāh Allāh, Allāh Allāh.* When we say, "*Bismillāhi 'r-Raḥmāni 'r-Raḥīm,*" we receive the power.

---

[11] Sūrat as-Saffāt, 37:173.

I don't know anything and I don't claim to know, but the mercy of the *Bismillāh* rains on me. There are clouds in the sky that say, "I am nothing," but it makes the mercy of rain. Without receiving the order, "O cloud, water this Earth!" it does not rain even a drop. *Allāhu Akbar*! Allāh ﷻ makes millions of tons of water wander in the sky to fall as rain, as hail or snow over wherever He ﷻ likes.

O foolish ones! Why don't you ask Who does this? You don't ask because the one who asks is reasonable, he is human, and the one who doesn't ask, who doesn't seek but only asks for barley is not human, he is an animal. *Amān, yā Rabbī*[12]*! Tawbah, yā Rabbī*[13]*!*

Our Creator Expects Us to Learn

To teach us, to inform us about our humanity and the honor of our humanity, the Lord of Heavens, our Allāh, our *Subḥān*, created us so that we know. He says, "Don't be ignorant, learn." And what should you learn? You should learn what is beneficial for you. There were so many *maktabs*[14], but in the new style of schools they teach nature and, "You should praise that one and curse that one." Okay, then who should you praise? First, you should say, "*Bismillāhi 'r-Raḥmāni 'r-Raḥīm.* All praise is to You! All praise is to You!" It praises Allāh Almighty, although He is not in need of being praised: He in His Own Being is *Ḥamīdun Majīd*!

You should teach, "Who created you?" to have familiarity and acquaintance with Him. The people of this time have no acquaintance with Allāh, not at all! They are acquainted with donkeys, with those who are foolish like themselves, but there is no one left who is acquainted with His Lord.

In earlier times they said, "You should take a hand," meaning, you should find beautiful servants who know the Lord of Heavens and Earth, who keep His orders, so that you take their hand and say, "O, servant who is honored with his Lord's service, save us too!" This was the meaning of 'taking a hand,' and now there is no one taking a hand and because they don't do this, they are taken by floods. Neither the Turks, the Arabs, the

[12] Protect us, O my Lord!

[13] I repent, O my Lord!

[14] A traditional Turkish school.

Americans, the Russians, nor the Chinese can do anything because they fell into such a crisis, into such a dangerous situation that no one can reach them.

ꕥ

Hold Fast to the Rope of Allāh

Abu Jahl, the uncle of our Prophet ﷺ, wanted to make him leave the world, meaning, "Let him die and we will be saved from him." Abu Jahl had a well dug in front of his door and he imprisoned himself at home, saying, "I am sick." He rested in his bed and had a well dug in front of his door and covered its surface so that whoever came would fall into it; he thought of this with his small mind.

He put his wooden bed in his room next to the window and he spread the news by saying, "Tell people that Abu Jahl is sick." Why did he do that? He used to say about the Prophet ﷺ, "He is an orphan." He is the Master of the Universe, so how can you call him an 'orphan'? But his mind was only very small. He said, "I got sick and that orphan goes to visit sick people. I had a well dug in front of my door and covered its top lightly. The moment he steps on it, he will fall into the well and we will finish him."

Our Prophet ﷺ visited sick people. Why? He ﷺ said, "Maybe the sick person's heart is softened and he might accept faith, because he is afraid of death." So our Prophet ﷺ went to visit Abu Jahl also, saying, "Maybe he will come to faith."

Right when Prophet ﷺ reached that well, he was about to take one more step into it when Jibrīl ؏ came and said, "Return, O Muḥammad!" and our Prophet ﷺ returned without stepping in it.

Seeing this, Abu Jahl was surprised, saying, "Let me run after him and call him back." Then he, himself, fell into that well! He started crying for help.

Mushriks[15] came, saying, "What happened to our master? We can hear his voice, but we can't see him."

They searched and searched, until finally they saw he called from inside the well, which was not that tall, only the height of one or two men.

He said, "Take my hand and get me out of this!"

---

[15] Polytheist; one who associates partners with Allāh.

They stretched out their arms and he was within their reach, so they said, "Give us your hand."

He said, "I am reaching up, but your hands are not reaching! Bring a rope or something."

They brought a rope and stretched it out, and then Abu Jahl cried, "It is not reaching! I will be drowned in here!" They brought more rope and stretched it out. "It is not reaching! Find another rope." So they found another rope and threw it down to him. He said, "It is not reaching! It is not reaching and I am dying here! Look around the neighborhood, let them bring a rope and save me!" They brought all the ropes from seven neighborhoods and threw them down to him. Crazy Abu Jahl cried, "*Yahu*, it is not reaching!" They stretched out all the ropes they had, but nothing could reach him!

Finally Abu Jahl said, "O my soldiers, even if you bring me all the ropes in the world they won't reach, but bring him to me." He often called Prophet ﷺ "the orphan of Abu Talib." *Astaghfirullāh*, he did not speak to Prophet ﷺ with respect. He said, "Bring me the orphan of Abu Talib, because no one except him can get me out."

Our Prophet, *Sulṭān al-Anbīyā*[16] ﷺ, O my beautiful Prophet!

So they called our Prophet ﷺ, *Sulṭān al-Anbīyā, Habībullāh*, who said, "Let me go and see what he will say to me." Prophet ﷺ went and said, "O Abu Jahl, will you come to faith if I take you out?"

He said, "I will, just take me out!"

"Give me your hand," Prophet ﷺ said and pulled him out.

Abu Jahl said, "I have never seen a greater magician than you!"

Our Prophet ﷺ—*SubḥānAllāh, SulṭānAllāh*, what a beautiful Prophet he is, with such a great character!—looked at him and replied, "It is up to you (to accept or reject faith)."

The crisis that today's people have fallen into is like this. They say, "Let's change this, let's put this law, let's do this to be saved from that

[16] King of the Prophets.

crisis." Even if you had wealth that was ten times bigger than America's treasury, it wouldn't be enough for you, still you will be left in that hole and you will die there. "Bring rope!" So they bring ropes from America and from Russia. "We are populists, we are on the left." Bring the ones who are on the right and on the left to get you out in the arena if you can, but seven treasuries like America's can't take you out!

Allāh Almighty says:

وَاعْتَصِمُوا بِحَبْلِ اللهِ جَمِيعًا وَلَا تَفَرَّقُوا

Hold fast to Allāh's rope and don't separate.[17]

Hold fast, all of you together, to the unbreaking rope of Allāh! "Hold your tongue and I will save you from that crisis." We have become like this now. They have fallen into such a hole that neither their laws nor their money can reach them. What money is it? For 700 years the Ottomans minted gold coins and they were the high state, but you didn't like the Ottomans and kicked them out. Their last sulṭān ruled for forty years and everyone had gold and silver in his pocket. Did you mint a single gold coin?

How to Avoid Global Crises

Every country has fallen into such a crisis that they can't get out of it; none of the measures they take is enough. It is not only our country, but the countries of the whole world, even small countries are all in the same situation and they can't be saved. Of course you can't be saved, you have to hold the Prophet's hand ﷺ[18]!

O Glorious Prophet! With the permission of your Lord ﷻ send us a sulṭān who will rule us and save us from the hands of tyrants! We should pull ourselves together, we should know our servanthood and try to make our *Akhirah* prosperous, this is it. The one who doesn't say, "*Bismillāhi 'r-Raḥmāni 'r-Raḥīm*" cannot find any goodness! He will be burned, destroyed, fall into miseries and perish. Hang the *Bismillāh* high as fire does not burn the place where it is, so take care. Earthquakes don't destroy it, floods don't carry it away. Take care!

---

[17] Sūrat Āli-'Imrān, 3:103.

[18] Practice his ways, his Sunnah.

O our Lord! You are *Subḥān*, You are *Sulṭān*! I say *tawbah* for myself and we also repent for Your servants. *Tawbah, yā Rabbī!* O our Lord! May You forgive us. Send us a sulṭān. *Tawbah yā Rabbī, tawbah yā Rabbī!* "What will you do with a sulṭān?" Now everyone thinks of himself as sulṭān (ruler) and they make a podium and all who climb it speak like a sulṭān, and what work do they achieve? Nothing, nothing! Do they ever do any work?

Wa min Allāhi 't-tawfīq. O you who think so highly of yourself! Keep this advice, because if you fall into punishment there is no shaykh or anyone from the *Awlīyā* who can save you, only the power of the Prophet ﷺ can save! Show respect for the Prophet! He is the *Khalif* of Allāh Almighty on Earth, *khalīfatullāh*[19]. Be careful and watch your mouth, or then a slap will come on your mouth, your mouth will reach your ears and you will be left like that.

They told a very famous person, "You can't enter here," but he insisted and said, "No, I will see."

"No, you can't enter here!"

That one, who thought highly of himself, said "No!" Whatever his occupation was, he insisted, "No, I have to enter and see the holy relics."

"No! Don't enter."

"I will enter."

Finally they said, "Okay, it is up to you, we won't interfere."

He took the first step, then the second step downstairs and on the third step there came a slap on his face that made his mouth go up to his ear.

He shouted, "What happened? Hold me!"

So they held him and pulled him up. His mouth was on his ear! They brought doctors who said, "This is not our job. His situation is normal in all aspects, but his mouth is on his ear. We don't have a medical field for this. Bring a holy person who can straighten his mouth and face."

So they brought a holy one, who came, took out his shoe, hit him on the face with it and he got straightened! Now should we wait like this, to be hit

[19] Allāh's vicegerent on Earth.

with a shoe for our mouth and face to be straightened? The shoe represents the wars. Avoid wars, as Allāh Almighty says:

وَالصُّلْحُ خَيْرٌ

And an amicable settlement is best.[20]

Peace is better, so try to make peace, Allāh ﷻ says, but they don't understand. Then suffer what comes on you!

May Allāh forgive us. All of us are sinners. What can we do? We should ask forgiveness from our Lord for the honor of His Beloved ﷺ. We hope that every owner of rights receives his right and *dunyā* finds its order.

Tawbah, yā Rabbī! Tawbah, yā Rabbī! Tawbah, yā Rabbī, astaghfirullāh! Shukr, yā Rabbī, shukr wa 'l-ḥamd, shukr wa 'l-ḥamd. Al-Fātiḥah.

This is a *ṣuḥbah* for the honor of the day of *Mawlid ash-Sharīf,* the day our Prophet ﷺ was born, and it is more than enough for seven countries. *Bismillāhi 'r-Raḥmāni 'r-Raḥīm. Al-Fātiḥah.*

If you don't know the *Fātiḥah,* then say *"Bismillāhi 'r-Raḥmāni 'r-Raḥīm"* and your task will succeed. Say *Bismillāh* for your every task and it will succeed, or you will be left as if your mouth is in your ear. *Tawbah, yā Rabbī! Tawbah, yā Rabbī! Tawbah, astaghfirullāh!*

O our Prophet ﷺ! May we be sacrificed in your way! Our ancestors were sacrificed in your way for a thousand years and they brought honor and glory. The Ottomans shook the world with their Sulṭānate. Now there are so many, maybe forty states that emerged from what the Ottomans ruled, but none of them can succeed. They claim to be inheritors of the Ottomans, but in reality, they didn't appreciate them and kicked them out, and they threw out the gold and took in the paper (currency), so they must suffer whatever comes on their heads!

ꕤ

[20] Sūrat an-Nisā, 4:128.

Science Can Never Replace Heavenly Knowledge

A*ʿūdhu billāhi min ash-shayṭāni 'r-rajīm. Bismillāhi 'r-Raḥmāni 'r-Raḥīm. Ash-hadu 'ana Muḥammadan abduhu wa rasūluh. Allāhumma salli wa sallim wa barik 'ala Sayyīdinā Muḥammadin wa ʿalā ālihi wa barik was sallam. Hū. Lā ilāha illa-Llāh. Aʿūdhu billāhi min ash-shayṭāni 'r-rajīm. Bismillāhi 'r-Raḥmāni 'r-Raḥīm. Lā hawla wa lā quwatta illa billāhi 'l-ʿAliyyu 'l-ʿAdhīm.*

May Allāh bless you and forgive me. We are thanking Allāh Almighty once again for granting us once again to reach this holiest month. The month of Ramaḍān is the "Month of Mercy." *Marhaban ahlan wa sahlan ya shahr ar-raḥmah!* Greeting and welcome, O month of mercy!

Madad, yā Sulṭān al-Anbīyā ﷺ, support us, O King of Prophets! We are meeting here for the honor of the beloved Prophet of the Lord, Allāh Almighty, whom He sent to His servants, Sayyīdinā Muḥammad ﷺ. May Allāh give him more honor here and Hereafter. He is the Most Respected, Most Honored One among all Mankind! He is beloved, Sayyīdinā Muḥammad ﷺ!

We shall look throughout this holy month at what will be granted daily to our people, to our brothers and sisters, the true *mu'mināt*. We are in need of some knowledge. You have science, what Mankind thinks in their heads from science fields, which will never be an ocean of knowledge, but divine knowledge is an ocean! We can say "divine knowledge," but we are not saying "divine science," as science will never be divine! Divine knowledge opens divine wisdoms.

People think according to science, and the fruit of science is technology. Therefore, one after one is falling in depression and technology can't take people out of depression. There is no treatment for Mankind through science, not for their troubles, depression, suffering, miseries, or from their problems! The only answer for their problems is through heavenly knowledge; one may treat Mankind's sufferings and miseries with heavenly knowledge and nothing else. Don't think that pills, tablets, or spirits "cure" people; it is impossible! Don't think that drugs may give people confidence, satisfaction, pleasure and happiness. Never!

Therefore, we are saying now Mankind needs knowledge that comes from Heavens through prophets, through illuminated people. When that knowledge comes, they will become enlightened and illuminated. You must know if everything is alright or not. When lights are coming, people are illuminated, like the beam of a flashlight. If heavenly knowledge comes to a person, it must show itself through space. If you can see that light and you must understand that heavenly knowledge is running through that one's heart.

We are in need of such knowledge, to arrange our inner lives and to be able to fix our relations from Earth to Heavens. As long as we are on Earth without a connection to Heavens, we are like other creatures with no value. There is value for Mankind as long as they may reach to Heavens. All prophets came from Heavens, but they lived on Earth to make our connections to Heavens easy. If they did not come from Heavens no one would be able to reach Heavens! And also after prophets, there must be someone whose connection is to Heavens, and if anyone is asking to reach Heavens then everyone has a heavenly station.

The Creator granted to everyone, women and men, divine stations in Heavens, and all of Heavens are in the Divine Presence. The Lord created Mankind and granted them their heavenly stations in the Divine Presence. What we are speaking about is knowledge from Heavens that reached to prophets, and traditional knowledge belongs to Heavens; what we are saying belongs to those heavenly oceans. Don't ask to try it by scientific methods; that will never give proof for knowledge. Science is on Earth and true knowledge is in Heavens. Science arranges your life on Earth, and heavenly knowledge arranges your heavenly life. Knowledge surrounds all science, which is a drop from the oceans of knowledge.

The Genuine Equality of Men and Women

Therefore, when a person enters Knowledge Oceans he or she finds confidence and pleasure, but science makes him in a very short distance; it imprisons people! We are in need of those heavenly connections and have been offered a way to reach our heavenly stations, where everyone's names are written on their individual, private, special stations: "That is for this one, that is for that one." There, men and women are equal. Here on Earth, they are asking for equality between men and women. Women are asking to be equal to men here in this life, but the Creator has distinguished characteristics of men and women.

If a male person uses his characteristics as a male, he will be a different creature from a woman using her characteristics as a male, which is a strange creature. Therefore, Allāh Almighty created a man to be a man and a woman to be a woman. If He Almighty was asking them to be equal, He would create everyone to be only men or only women! He created men and women, two kinds, and each one is independent in their creation. There is no equality in their creation, but as human beings all of them are the same, all are servants, and servanthood is making them equal in the Divine Presence.

But now women are asking for another kind of equality, which is foolish, useless, and has no value. Their real equality is through their servanthood in the Divine Presence and Allāh Almighty is asking for men and women to perfect their servanthood! Allāh Almighty is asking all human beings to be servants, and servanthood is the true equality among men and women. All of them have been offered to be servants, and there is no higher honor than to be servants to the Lord, Allāh Almighty.

But now women think if they do man's work it will be an honor for them. They are becoming engineers, soldiers. They think that is an honor for them because men are doing all these things and they are asking, "Why are we not doctors or engineers? We must be!" That is short-mindedness that results from small thinking. They do not understand what Allāh Almighty is giving to all Mankind. The highest honor is to be His servant! His Majesty, the King, sulṭāns, emperors, all of them are proud to be accepted by the Lord, Allāh Almighty as His servant.

Her Majesty, Queen Elizabeth, may Allāh bless her, is proud to be a servant of the Church of England. She refers to herself as "servant." Emperors were also servants and in Islam, all of them were servants of the Lord, Allāh Almighty. They never knew any higher rank and Allāh grants them equality by making all of them His servants.

But now women are fighting, saying, "Why can't we be equal with men?" You can't be like men because you were created women and you have been honored to be His servant, finished!

The Unique Honor of Women

What promise did the mother of Sayyida Maryam[21] ﷺ make to Allāh? All of you must know it. In *Sūrat Āli 'Imrān*[22], the lady of the Family of ʿImrān prayed when she was pregnant, "That which I am carrying, I shall give in Jerusalem as a servant of the Lord, Allāh Almighty." She thought it would be a son. The Holy Qur'an gives every evidence for women and men to be fully confident of their positions in Heavens! We are speaking from knowledge, not from my stomach or from my head, but from my heart! She asked for what she was carrying to be the Lord's servant. When she gave birth, she was very surprised, saying, "O my Lord! What happened? I can't keep my promise as I have a daughter," and she thought to throw it away, but Allāh Almighty gave an example for all Mankind, saying, "No, I am accepting her as a servant in *Bayt al-Muqqadas* (the Holy House in Jerusalem)." That means Allāh Almighty is honoring all women, accepting them as a servant, just as a son is accepted!

That girl, Sayyida Maryam ﷺ, was accepted, which is divine equality, but women are fighting that honor. No woman must be like a man or work like a man as that is not equality! Allāh Almighty honored men to be men and women to be women! Keep the ownership of servanthood! Both wings of men and of women must keep the honor of each other: men must keep the honor of women and women must keep the honor of men. In particular, men must keep the honor of women as their equals in honor and respect!

Allāh Almighty is giving women a little bit more power for this life, to carry the burden of life, because your creation is stronger. They are weak, but they are stronger than men in worshiping and they will easily reach a connection to their heavenly stations. Now it is possible for men to reach a connection in forty days, but we may do the same for women in forty hours! If I say an order to a man, he must keep it for forty days to maintain a connection, but for women I may do it for forty hours, to reach a connection. Then you will look up and wonder, "Where are they!"

So the sole discussion of the true equality of men and women is based on heavenly knowledge, but philosophers and scientists may continue on their knowledge. Knowledge gives confidence to hearts, and thanks to Allāh

[21] The Holy Mother of Jesus Christ, whose details are narrated in the Holy Qur'ān.

[22] The third chapter of Holy Qur'ān.

Almighty that He granted for our first meeting *sakinah*, the deepest peace, which brings confidence and *insha'Allāh* that will open in your hearts.

O Mankind! We are in need of that deep peace in our hearts because difficult conditions are covering Mankind, who is now losing balance in their spiritual beings. May Allāh grant us through these Endless Oceans what He granted to His Beloved One ﷺ and His *Awlīyā*, that we may perhaps complete forty days or forty hours, that we may reach the Holy Night of Power in Holy Ramaḍān! May Allāh grant you good understanding and grant me to speak on divine wisdoms.

Allāh Allāh, Allāh Allāh, Allāh Allāh, 'Azīz Allāh!

Allāh Allāh, Allāh Allāh, Allāh Allāh, Karīm Allāh!

Allāh Allāh, Allāh Allāh, Allāh Allāh, Subḥān Allāh!

Allāh Allāh, Allāh Allāh, Allāh Allāh, Sulṭān Allāh!

Fātiḥah.

By the Name of Allāh Almighty, *alḥamdulillāh*, this is the holy month of Ramaḍān, and Heavens are open for the servants of the Lord, Allāh Almighty, and the doors of Paradise are open for the servants of Allāh. Hells are locked up, not to be open for the servants of the *ummah*. May Allāh Almighty grant us and the nation of Muḥammad ﷺ from His endless Mercy Oceans, from His endless Favor Oceans.

We are expecting our Lord's blessings! There is an important point to be well known: Allāh Almighty created human beings, and they are His servants and also His deputies, and Allāh Almighty is granting His divinely love to all His creatures. To which kind of people is Allāh Almighty granting from His divinely love? He created all with His love, but He will make it more and more.

Our True Servanthood Precedes This Physical Life

Allāh Almighty sent His servants to this life, but do you think it was for *dunyā*, just to be servants of this world? If a believer is thinking this, it must be wrong. Allāh Almighty never sent His servants here to this life to be servants for this *dunyā*, but for them to be aware of the pre-Eternal[23], that they are not servants only here. No one knows when their soul was created except the Creator; however, don't think that your existence began when you were born in this life! Our physical being in this life began by dust, but only Allāh Almighty knows when your true existence began. From pre-Eternal, His servants were servants and you were one of those servants! We were all servants from pre-Eternal up to Eternal[24], and Allāh Almighty gave honor to you through that creation, by making you His servant and then the Almighty gave you a new physical being. Your real being is in the Divinely Presence, but He gave you a physical being here, then He observed when He dressed you in your physical body, are you going to lose or forget your servanthood? That is important, and the biggest test for Mankind.

Mankind was created a long time ago, before "time" and "space" began, when there was no time and Mankind was in the Divinely Presence as servants to their Lord, Allāh Almighty. His Divinely Will asked to dress them in a physical body and send them to this life. I am not speaking from science; we are speaking from heavenly knowledge, and there can be no objecting on it. You must listen and obey! What we are saying is from heavenly knowledge and only a few people are authorized to speak from real knowledge in our days. You are lucky to be listening and accepting what we are saying to you!

The Lord, Allāh Almighty, ordered Mankind to be dressed in a physical body that He created in Paradise, from where we all observed how Creation was happening. All Mankind saw what Allāh Almighty created for them of their physical being or physical body, then His Divinely Will asked for a big test for them, and divine wisdoms granted endless blessings on those to be dressed with a physical being. From that time up to today, and up to the end of the Day of Resurrection, the Last Day, that divine test continues. Divine people are asking for equality between two kinds of human beings, women and men. Can anyone say who is truly preferred in the Divine Presence, women or men?

---

[23] Azalīyun, The Eternal; a state of existence before this universe was created.

[24] Abadīyun, the Everlasting; Eternity; Eternal Life.

The Remedy for All Your Troubles

Tawbah, yā Rabbī! Tawbah, astaghfirullāh! Tawbah, yā Rabbī! Tawbah, astaghfirullāh! Let us say, "*Bismillāhi 'r-Raḥmāni 'r-Raḥīm.*" The remedy for all your troubles is *Bismillāhi 'r-Raḥmāni 'r-Raḥīm.* What opens every closed door is *Bismillāhi 'r-Raḥmāni 'r-Raḥīm.* The Dominions of Heavens and Earth stand with *Bismillāhi 'r-Raḥmāni 'r-Raḥīm.*

When you say "*Bismillāhi 'r-Raḥmāni 'r-Raḥīm,*" it can stop the running waters. What will stop the floods is not this or that measure. If one sincere servant of Allāh says, "*Bismillāhi 'r-Raḥmāni 'r-Raḥīm.* O flood! Don't come on us, go another way!" even if a mountain is ripped apart and the flood passes through it, it won't touch those Believers!

Tawbah, yā Rabbī! Tawbah, yā Rabbī! Al-Fātiḥah.

May the *barakah*[25] of the *Bismillāh* come upon your generations. Teach your children, "O Believers! Say, '*Bismillāhi 'r-Raḥmāni 'r-Raḥīm,*'" and Shayṭān must stay away from them!

May Allāh ﷻ grant me some strength so I can do something also, as I am left helpless. O Allāh, forgive me! Forgive me and send Your servants who will bring these servants to the path of forgiveness. O Lord, send us a sulṭān! *Bismillāhi 'r-Raḥmāni 'r-Raḥīm.*

---

[25] Blessing.

Why People Are So Tired

As-salāmu ʿalaykum. You must keep some advices a little bit; if you are not able to keep all of them, we must try to keep some.

Marhaban bikum, "Welcome to you!" *Marhaban* for whom? You may say, *marhaban, marhaban, yā shahr as-siyām*, Welcome, welcome, O the Month of Fasting! *Marhaban, marhaban, yā shahr al-qiyām*, Welcome, welcome, O the Month of Standing in Supplication! *Marhaban, marhaban, yā shahr al-ghufrān*, Welcome, welcome, O the Month of Forgiveness! *Marhaban, marhaban*!

O Believers! Change your direction in this holiest of the twelve months, don't make this holy month as other holy months or ordinary months. Holy Ramaḍān has a specialty from which heavenly beings and angels become happy, happier and happiest in this holy month!

What is that reason to be the holiest month? O Salafi *ʿulamas*, say what is the reason that *shahr ar-Ramaḍān*, the holy month of Ramaḍān, has a special status among other months? Make it clear for the servants of our Lord. All of us are servants and that is our highest honor we have been granted from our Lord, Almighty Allāh, to be His servants. Servanthood is the most highly respected level for all Mankind and all nations, beginning from Adam ﷺ to the Seal of All prophets, Sayyīdinā Muḥammad ﷺ.

To Forget Divine Orders and Follow One's Ego is Exhausting

O People! Who is working for Allāh ﷻ will never be tired. You are tiring daily, but why are you tiring, do you know? O Salafi *ʿulamas*! Why are you not saying to people why they are tiring? Answer! I am asking, what is the answer for that question? For what reason is Mankind tiring? That is an important point. Say clearly to your *mulūk* (kings), shaykhs, rich ones, and those who are tiring, "For what are you tiring?" Kings and leaders are also tiring, but which thing is making them tired? Say, you *ʿulama* that are running to be Wahhabi ones on the wrong way!

Before, kings and leaders took much care and became more pleased by the celebration of the birthday of the Seal of Prophets, Sayyīdinā Muḥammad ﷺ, but now Wahhabi people are around them, saying, "O Sulṭān! That is *bidʿa*. Don't do it, leave it, leave it." That is their advice and kings and other leaders are slowly, slowly, slowly making that celebration not to be seen and not to be heard, making the birthday of the Seal of Prophets ﷺ as an ordinary day. No!!!

O Salafi *ʿulamas*! You advise your kings and leaders not to make a birthday celebration for the Seal of Prophets ﷺ, but you say nothing when they celebrate birthdays of their children! No one is saying, "That is *bidʿa,* that is not correct," but to make a celebration for the Seal of Prophets ﷺ they are saying, "No, it is not correct." For this reason, Allāh Almighty will send on your head such pain that no physician may relieve, such tremendous pain that you will drink a full bottle of pain tablets, but it will not stop because you are such people against the Most Glorified One in the Divinely Presence, Sayyīdinā Muḥammad ﷺ! (Mawlana Shaykh stands and sits.) You are running for that birthday celebration, saying, "O congratulations and long life and long happiness for His Highness, the Crown Prince (Her Highness, the Crown Princess)!"

O Salafi *ʿulamas*! Allāh Almighty will send on you such pain on your head that no one will find a way to stop! That is suitable for you, then you will understand what is the true way and what is the wrong way. You will understand! Give your most high honor and glorifying for the Seal of Prophets, *Sayyidi 'l-Awwalīn wa 'l-ʿĀkhirīn* ﷺ! Why are you tiring, say to your people!

O Salafi *ʿulamas*, beware! Hear, listen, and keep heavenly advising. Which thing is making a person tired, say to the people! You can't say. We may say *bi ʿidhnillāh*[26], that is because you are not doing everything for your Lord's pleasure, you are following your egos, to make your egos happy. If anyone is running to make his ego happy, that effort, that work is making you tired. Everything that is not for the sake of the Lord of Heavens is a heavy burden on the shoulders of kings, queens, princes, princesses, governors, presidents, and so on.

O People! You must know why you are getting tired. People are not working for Allāh *Subḥānahu wa Taʿalā Rabba ʿama yushrikūn,* "Glory be to Allāh, Who is above what they ascribe to Him." Which thing is making people tired? You must understand and you must ask to Azhar ash-Sharīf

---

[26] By Allāh Almighty's leave; with His permission.

ʿulamas, doctors of Shariʿah, *ʿulamas,* and Salafi *ʿulamas,* why are people tiring? Normally, human beings will never be tired.

Our Prophet was Never Tired!

O Salafi *ʿulamas*! Say, if at any time on any day or at any hour the Seal of Prophets ﷺ said, "I am tired." Say! He never said it. Are any *Ḥadīth* books writing that Prophet ﷺ said, "I am tired." He was never tired! But we are tiring, including myself also, and I am asking forgiveness. Anyone who is working for Allāh ﷻ is never tiring. The whole Muslim world and humanity must know that if they are working for Allāh, they will never be tired, they will always be like giants, powerful! Their hands are powerful, their bodies are powerful, their heads are powerful and every organ is powerful!

I must say this because kings, princes, shaykhs, and rich ones are all tiring. If a man is tiring that means every organ from him is tiring, never making *Shahādah*[27], always down. This is a good understanding, O shaykhs and *mulūk*, because you are not doing for Allāh; therefore, your organs are weakened. If you are working for Allāh, you will never be tired, like the Seal of Prophets ﷺ, but your tent pole has just broken down. You may run to the east and to the west to find a cure, but you can't find it, because if you are tiring, every organ is tiring, finished.

When you are tiring, you must understand the cause. Where are you, O Salafi *ʿulamas?* Say this to people in Arabic, in Turkish, in Persian, and in Urdu. People are tiring because they are not living for Allāh, because they are not working for Allāh, because they are agents of Shayṭān, because they are working for Shayṭān, and they will be tired here and Hereafter!

May Allāh forgive us. That is an important point. *Allāh, Allāh. Allāh, Allāh.* Therefore, I am making *duʿa* for those who are tired but coming against me, such that doctors from the east to the west can't find any cure for them. Don't assault me! I am sometimes an easy one, but sometimes I am a very hard, difficult one.

This is a celebration *khutbah* that may be a declaration for the honor of the holy month. *Ramaḍān Mubarak, Ramaḍān Karīm*! If you are not listening, you are eating and you will be tiring; by halfway you will be tired. Take

---

[27] Creed of Faith.

care, O kings, shaykhs, rich ones, *princes* and others. If you are asking to always be in *haqq* and in power, try to do everything for Allāh, and you will never become tired.

Therefore, they are making me say to you, to ask if the Seal of Prophets ﷺ said, "O, I am tired." Which *Ḥadīth*? No! Beware of a heavenly cursing, heavenly punishment! Do everything for Allāh and you will never be tired. You may be 90 or 100 years, but you will not be tired. You may be 18, 20, 25 but if you are not working for Allāh ﷻ, you will be tired. Your physical being will be melting, melting. That is the reason for countless hospitals and for countless shaykhs, princes, kings and presidents entering them. For what? For visiting, because they are feeling, "We are tiring. O my doctor, can you find any new medicine? Take away my inability. Please sir, you must check." Finished! You are tired because you lived for Shayṭān, not for *ar-Raḥmān*[28], so you will be melted, finished!

May Allāh forgive us. *Amān, yā Rabbī!*

Tonight is the first night of the holy month of Ramaḍān. Try to do everything for Allāh, then you will not be hungry, angry, thirsty, or tired. Give and take; if you are not giving for Allāh, you can't take anything back!

May Allāh forgive me and forgive you, also.

Fātiḥah.

[28] The All-Merciful; Allāh ("The One God").

Divine Mercy Will Shower You!

B*ismillāhi 'r-Raḥmāni 'r-Raḥīm*! Unfortunately the whole world, the Muslim world also, has forgotten to say, *"Bismillāhi 'r-Raḥmāni 'r-Raḥīm"*. Allāh Almighty, *Jalla Jalāluhu,* created the Holy Pen and from the Greatness of His Glance upon it, the Nib of the Pen cracked.

The Pen asked, "What should I write, O Lord?"

He ﷻ said, "Write, '*Bismillāhi 'r-Raḥmāni 'r-Raḥīm.*'"

Bismillāhi 'r-Raḥmāni 'r-Raḥīm! O our Lord! Do not make us from those who forget the *Bismillāh*; let us be remolded with the *Bismillāh,* then we will be decent ones!

"What should I write, O Lord?"

When Allāh Almighty looked upon it with His Greatness, the Nib of the Pen opened and the Ink came out. May we stand up with the *Bismillāh* and sit with the *Bismillāh,* what a great honor.

He ﷻ said, "Write, '*Bismillāhi 'r-Raḥmāni 'r-Raḥīm.*'"

كل أمر ذي بال لا يبدأ فيه ببسم الله الرحمن الرحيم فهو أقطع أو (فهو ابتر)

Any action which does not begin with 'Bismillāhi 'r-Raḥmāni 'r-Raḥīm' is cut off; it has no continuity.[29]

Is it not the *Ḥadīth*? Whatever act starts without the *Bismillāh* is cut off, it is of no use. They removed the *Bismillāh,* they forgot it. *Allāh, Allāh*! Then, some narrations say that seven-hundred years passed until the Holy Pen wrote, *"Bismillāhi 'r-Raḥmāni 'r-Raḥīm."* The *Bismillāh* should be made known to the people, so put the *Bismillāh* on your doors, in your homes, in your offices, in your cars and have no fear! Even if the world becomes upside-down, that person will have no fear. *Allāh, Allāh*! *Allāhu Akbar*, how beautiful! Therefore, let them say the *Bismillāh* at least forty times daily, let them recite it. The best is to recite the *Bismillāh* 100 times daily, then the blessings and mercy flow like a rushing river!

---

[29] (Aḥmad, al-Musnad).

What should we do? They write many books about this, but they can't say as they don't know the essence of the matter. This informs to recite the *Bismillāh* for every matter. In the past, every book began with *Bismillāhi 'r-Raḥmāni 'r-Raḥīm,* for *ta'zīm* (respect). You can't finish the miracles of the *Bismillāh* even if you write loads of books. *Allāhu Akbar al-Akbar*!

O Lord! May You forgive us. O Lord! May You forgive us. O Lord! May You send to us Your holy servants who will teach us these things as we are left bewildered. *Tawbah, yā Rabbī*[30]! *Tawbah, yā Rabbī*!

For this they took children to the *maktab,* a traditional school, to the presence of the headmaster, with a big crowd accompanying them. They made it a ceremony, and the headmaster first taught the children, "Say, '*Bismillāhi 'r-Raḥmāni 'r-Raḥīm. Rabbī yassir wa lā tu'assir. Rabbī tammim bi 'l-khayr.* O Allāh, make it easy and not difficult! O Allāh, let this bring goodness!'"

What a beautiful beginning and *adab,* from which mercy showered them! Now we are under the manifestation of Allāh's wrath. I seek refuge from it! I seek refuge from it! I seek refuge from it! I seek refuge from it, O Allāh, O Lord! May You send us a master of the people who should teach these things. Before, every neighborhood mosque had a room where the Hoja Effendi[31] taught children to read and write Arabic and the Holy Qur'ān. If one needed further education, they attended *madrassahs,* religious schools, in which every child knew the *Bismillāh*! Now people are raised without the *Bismillāh* and they became without it. Who forgets the *Bismillāh* will be forgotten and there is not even a drop of heavenly support for them, and even if they bury him in gold, still he will get up[32] with his hands empty!

The Two Blind Men

There was a king, Sulṭān Maḥmūd, who often had a chicken or duck stuffed with gold and sent out to be given to whoever called, "O Lord! *Yā Ma'būd,* O

---

[30] I repent, Oh my Lord!

[31] Title of Turkish origin for a man of high education or social standing in a Mediterranean or Arab country; analogous to Esquire, junior to Bey in Egypt.

[32] On Resurrection Day, he will rise.

Worshipped One[33]!" and, "*Yā* Maḥmūd!" So they gave it to two men, both of whom were blind.

We may say, "*Bismillāhi 'r-Raḥmāni 'r-Raḥīm,*" as whoever remembers the Name of Allāh first, Allāh makes his every doing easy for him. How beautiful that Allāh straightens the work of the one who says, "Allāh," and the work of who doesn't say it is totally corrupt.

One day when Sulṭān Maḥmūd was passing through a place, he saw two blind men sitting together. One of them was saying, "*Yā Maʿbūd! Yā Maʿbūd!*" and the other one was saying, "*Yā* Maḥmūd! *Yā* Maḥmūd! *Yā* Maḥmūd!" Both were beggars who lived on what people gave.

So Sulṭān Maḥmūd said to his men, "Fill a chicken with gold and send it to that one who says, '*Yā* Maḥmūd,'" and they gave it.

That one looked at it and said, "O friend! They brought me something like a chicken, but I am full. Give me a few coins and I will give it to you and you can eat it."

The second one discovered it was a chicken. He gave a few coins and took it, then he saw that it was full of gold. He took it to his house and came back again and sat.

The first one said (in a weak voice), "*Yā* Maḥmūd! *Yā* Maḥmūd! *Yā* Maḥmūd!" The second one's work had succeeded, so he cried out very strongly, "*Yā Maʿbūd! Yā Maʿbūd! Yā Maʿbūd!*"

"What happened to them?" the sulṭān asked.

"That one who says, '*Yā* Maḥmūd,' again calls, '*Yā* Maḥmūd,' and the other one calls, "*Yā Maʿbūd!*" in a strong voice."

Then the sulṭān filled a duck with gold and sent it to the one calling, "*Yā* Maḥmūd!"

He again looked it over, saying, "O my friend! They brought me something similar again, but I am full. Whatever you can do, give me its equivalent and take this."

[33] One of the Ninety-nine Beautiful Names of God.

The other one was ready from the previous time so again he checked and found it full. He said, "Take this, I will give you more this time." He took it and left that place and went to his home.

Sulṭān Maḥmūd investigated what happened.

His men said, "The situation is the same."

He said, "Okay, bring me that one who says, 'Yā Maḥmūd.'" They brought him and he said, "O poor servant of Allāh! You are calling to me and I granted you gifts so many times, but you are still begging there." He then said to his men, "Take this one to my treasury, put a shovel in his hand and whatever amount he shovels, give it to him!"

So they took him to the treasury and the sulṭān was watching. They said to him, "Take this shovel and dig."

That poor one could not see, so he held the shovel from the wrong end and when he shoveled only a few coins were caught.

Then Sulṭān Maḥmūd said (a famous saying) , *vermezse Maʿbūd, neylesin Maḥmūd*, "If *Maʿbūd* does not grant, what can Maḥmūd do?"

People are now like this: they are not calling to Allāh, they are not calling to Allāh! Rather, they say, "We will do business, we will study, we will do this and that (to make our own way)." You make a mess, finished! Such people have become zero. Our ancestors' majesty is lost and still that one who calls to Maḥmūd, who calls to *dunyā*, calls to Shayṭān, still he is all alone, having nothing! They hold the shovel by the wrong end and no one has money in his pocket! For forty years, the Ottoman Sulṭāns ruled a state that was seven times greater than Turkey is now and every one had gold in his pocket, but now people have paper in their pockets! This is the power of a sulṭān and this is the work of other imitated states. They don't even have paper in their pockets; they can't even provide enough paper for the people, let alone gold. That sulṭān was with Allāh ﷻ and these are with Shayṭān, the whole world.

May Allāh forgive us.

Why Previous Contentment Vanished

Before, people were not obsessed with education like now. One went to the *maktab* and learn, and who wanted more knowledge went to the *madrassa*[34]. Now they have removed the *maktabs* and *madrassahs* and everywhere is full of new schools. They can't manage with the teachers as the huge government falls short of money to pay them. Maybe 100,000 teachers wait for payment, but this is of no use and even if you give them everything, they will still say, "We are hungry," because any work without the *Bismillāh* has no result, so they are like this.

Ours is the most high religion! Islam teaches everything, but they are not learning it and they are not teaching it. They go after Shayṭān, they worship him and forget Allāh, and because of this they are never saved from troubles or miseries. Even if the Turks' whole land was made of gold, still they would be left with the attribute of the poor beggar, because they don't say "Allāh." Okay, don't say it! The mercy taps are in the Heavens; *khayr* taps descend from the Heavens, but they look for them on the Earth, looking and looking, and what did they find? They found sewers and rats walking in filth!

They said, "How nice are these sewers, what a nice life this is with everywhere open, just as we like! Let's enter this sewer like these rats and wander around very happily." So they got in it and can't get out; they fell into the dirty life. Shame on them!

Allāhu Akbar. For forty years on his own, Sulṭān Abdul Hamid Han ruled, may Paradise be his abode. Everyone had gold in their pockets and now they don't even have paper (currency) in their pockets as Allāh *Jalla Jalāluhu* (said), "You leave Me and live for your ego. Take it! Who lives for Me, I provide them with everything."

Amān yā Rabbī, tawbah yā Rabbī, tawbah. Wa min Allāhi 't-tawfīq, bi hurmati 'l-Fātiḥah.

[34] Religious school.

Manifestations of Colors

B*ismillāhi 'r-Raḥmāni 'r-Raḥīm!* May we remember the Holy Name of our Lord. The *Bismillāh* has a majesty, a magnificence! The holy ones are making us speak a few words, and Shaykh Mehmet Effendi's *fayz*, spiritual energy, is strong. He receives, receives and may he receive and receive and be the joy and pride of Islam, and may you also be the soldiers of Mahdi ﷺ and carry his flags!

What do we expect from *dunyā*? For all these thousands of years, *dunyā* fed all these people; people lived, passed away and new ones came. The ones born before left and new ones came. We said, "*Bismillāhi 'r-Raḥmāni 'r-Raḥīm*," and stood up to show respect. Yes, even if a corporal[35] calls to a private[36], the private rushes to stand up straight to show respect. This is for the corporal, for the lowest rank, and for higher ranks he stands in astonishment! A man respects another man because he has a higher rank. We are human beings, we have understanding, intelligence. The respect a simple private shows a corporal, what a shame that today people can't show it for their Lord, Who created them! They don't think of standing up for two minutes for Him ﷻ, and then bow and making *sajda*[37]!

We are now it the Era of Ignorance; the ignorance before our Prophet ﷺ was the first and now this is the second, in which the whole world has become ignorant and they are fighting each other. Everywhere they invented an idol to make people forget Allāh ﷻ and they trick people in many ways. The ignorant people of this time want to bring everything down to their standard, they don't want anyone above their level or their standard, they want everyone to be below their level and now a person doesn't accept anyone above him. Innovation, and reforms caused the misery people suffer today. First of all, they made people forget the *Bismillāh* and now no one says it. Shame on them!

If you ask, "Who created you?" they answer, "Nature?" This has no benefit, my son! Before, in the old times people made statues and

---

[35] A low level military rank.

[36] A soldier of the lowest military rank.

[37] Part of the ritual prayer, salāt.

worshipped them and Arabs had the idol, Hubal, right? Abu Jahl called, "Long live glorious Hubal!" It was their biggest, greatest idol and they called to it like that. However, before battle the People of Islam called, *"Allāhu Akbar! Allāhu Akbar! Allāhu Akbar!"* and drew their swords and the tips of their swords sparkled!

Lā ilāha illa-Llāh Sayyīdinā Muḥammadun Rasūlullāh! Lā ilāha illa-Llāh Sayyīdinā Muḥammadun Rasūlullāh! Showing respect is the glory and honor of Mankind! To show respect for what is above us is our honor. The greatest glory is to say, *"Lā ilāha illa-Llāh Muḥammadun Rasūlullāh,"* and it is to say, *"Lā ilāha illa-Llāh."* We may stand up even a hundred or one-thousand times and the *nūr*[38] of that Holy Word penetrates into our beings. *Tūba thumma tūba*! Good tidings for those who know their Lord, who know their Creator and make service to Him. May Allāh not expel us from His Servanthood!

Ta'budunī! Allāh Almighty says, "Worship Me, serve Me!" but do the people of this time think? They don't, because the people of this time left their humanity and are running after the animal attributes. They don't respect or consider their spirituality, but want to do everything their egos ask from them; they left their humanity. Humanity is connected to the *Malakūt* on one side with our soul, and its other side is connected to *dunyā* with our ego. Whoever strengthens his spirituality will succeed.

How to Reveal the Power of Your Diamond

You know that diamonds are collected from under the ground among the coals. If a diamond is not cut it has no value. They first cut the diamond, then that diamond becomes suitable for the hands of sulṭāns. Now we are also, in this unrefined life of ours, like diamond stones that haven't been cut. It needs to be cut; it should be polished so that its gem appears.

Every person has a color. No one can know the number of colors, and there is a unique manifestation in each color. Every person's gem is different and if they work on it, their gem will appear. With what can you work on it? With the *Bismillāh*! Say, *"Bismillāhi 'r-Raḥmāni 'r-Raḥīm"* and your gem appears; if not, you are left in the ground among the rocks as a worthless stone. Say the *Bismillāh* so that your gem appears!

---

[38] Light.

Kullu muyassarun limā khuliqa lahu, Mankind has a place in the Creation with his humanity: Allāh Almighty appointed him as sulṭān on Earth and granted him Sulṭānate. Who is a sulṭān? It is he who brings out his gem! For us to bring out our gem, He ﷻ sent His Beloved to show His Way. He ﷻ says, "Polish him so his gem appears." What makes the gem in a person appear is to recite *"Bismillāhi 'r-Raḥmāni 'r-Raḥīm." Mashā'Allāh, Mashā'Allāh*! Now no one is trying to bring out his gem and they are left like rocks, they are not aware there is a gem inside them, but there is no other Creation higher than Man. *Asta'īdhu billāh:*

وَلَقَدْ كَرَّمْنَا بَنِي آدَمَ

We have honored the Children of Adam.[39]

"We granted the Children of Adam such a gem that no one can know its origin or its reality!" Only Allāh knows, and He ﷻ informed His Beloved up to the level he should know, then after the Prophet ﷺ He ﷻ grants to the *Awlīyā,* who work on this gem; He grants from that power and our gem opens. When our gem reveals, the ways of Paradise opens for us! What is the instrument that reveals our gem? It is *Bismillāhi 'r-Raḥmāni 'r-Raḥīm.* Say this and have no fear, thinking, "May we remember Your Name first, O Allāh!"

For this, the holy ones teach in the *Mawlid ash-Sharīf.* We should remember the Name of Allāh first so that our gem appears. Say "Allāh" and don't fear from their cannons or weapons or other rubbish things they make, simply say "Allāh" and He ﷻ makes them stop!

There are at least forty holy ones. If one of them says "Allāh," He can burn all of them! If one of them says *"Bismillāhi 'r-Raḥmāni 'r-Raḥīm,"* all of them (tyrants/oppressors) will flatten! What can the invented instruments of those impure unbelievers do? How can they reach the power we have? The power of the believer and of the saints of Allāh comes from Heavens. What brings the power from Heavens? *Bismillāhi 'r-Raḥmāni 'r-Raḥīm! Bismillāhi 'r-Raḥmāni 'r-Raḥīm! Bismillāhi 'r-Raḥmāni 'r-Raḥīm!* Say this and power comes on you!

---

[39] Sūrat al-'Isrā, 17:70.

Don't sleep, open your eyes! Get up saying *"Bismillāh,"* live saying *"Bismillāh,"* sleep saying *"Bismillāh,"* and wake up saying *"Bismillāh!"* What a beautiful companion, what a beautiful fellowship! Such a person suffers no troubles or illnesses!

Dogs Run after Bones: Be True Human Beings!

O our Lord, our *Subḥān*, our Sulṭān! You have so many servants that can teach us these ways for the honor of Your Beloved, but He ﷻ leaves us, saying, "Do as you like. Let us see if they will eat from the plate where dogs eat or from the table where men eat." Wherever you throw the bone, a dog runs after it. Our illustration is not wrong: a dog runs after the bone, it wants bone. Can Mankind ever run after a bone? What is *dunyā*? Why do you run after it? Why don't you run after the Orders of Allāh Almighty? Say, *"Bismillāhi 'r-Raḥmāni 'r-Raḥīm."* Whoever remembers Your Name, "O Allāh!" You make every work easy for that person.

Here, this is enough. Say, *"Bismillāhi 'r-Raḥmāni 'r-Raḥīm"* in your every work and Allāh makes it come easy. Get used to saying it, don't be left as an animal, but dress in the human rank! Animals have no thought other than eating and drinking. Who's only thought is eating and drinking has no value. He has no value! A chicken also scratches all day long. It never stops, never says, "I am full." A chicken always scratches the ground, always eats and never gets full. He eats from this side, excretes from the other side and then starts scratching again. Don't be like this: don't live to eat, don't live for pleasures, live to make service for Allāh Almighty and say, *"Bismillāhi 'r-Raḥmāni 'r-Raḥīm."*

O our Lord, forgive us and grant us strength! We want strength to serve You. The amount of life You appointed for us is in Your Hands, but we should complete this life of ours in an honored way, so when the angels take our soul, the Angel of Death, ʿAzra'īl ﷺ, the angels may be surprised when they come and say, "What a beautiful person with *nūr*, light! This one is with *Bismillāhi 'r-Raḥmāni 'r-Raḥīm."* Who is without the *Bismillāh* is ugly and everything without the *Bismillāh* is ugly!

كل أمر ذي بال لا يبدأ فيه ببسم الله الرحمن الرحيم فهو أقطع أو (فهو ابتر)

Any action which does not begin with 'Bismillāhi 'r-Raḥmāni 'r-Raḥīm' is cut off; it has no continuity.[40]

Whichever matter starts without the *Bismillāh* is *abtar*, cut off and no good comes from it. The people, the nations who forget the *Bismillāh* have no goodness in them and they fight each other, they fight each other! The world today is in the second part of the Ignorance Era and that is what they strive for.

You eat and then you will go to WC[41]. Is your occupation only this? Since you never make *sajda*, did they appoint you as the officer of WC? Say the *Bismillāh* and live for Allāh! *Bismillāhi 'r-Raḥmāni 'r-Raḥīm.*

O Arabs! O Turks! Some of them Egyptian, some of them Turkish, some of them from Iraq, all from different nations. No! Say, "believer," say, "Allāh's Servant!" Try to make service for Allāh. Say, '*Bismillāhi 'r-Raḥmāni 'r-Raḥīm*!" Be accustomed to this, O Arabs and Turks! Leave claiming to be Arabs or Turks and say, "I am Muslim."

May Allāh not separate us from Islam and not make us forget the *Bismillāh. Yā Rabbī*! We are left helpless, O Lord! Send us a Master who will teach us the *Bismillāh*.

I saw report cards of the children and on the back there is a full page of writing that neither I nor the children understand. Whoever is the owner of that writing, he also is a servant like you. Why don't you write on it the Name of Who Created you, "*Bismillāhi 'r-Raḥmāni 'r-Raḥīm.*" Why don't you teach them the *Bismillāh*? Allāh will ask them, "Why didn't you teach the children, My servants, My Holy Name? I will give you such a calamity that you can't be saved from it unless you say the *Bismillāh*!"

Say, "*Bismillāhi 'r-Raḥmāni 'r-Raḥīm*" daily from seven to forty times, or from forty to seventy times, or from seventy to one-hundred times and your heart will be at peace, your body will be in health and Allāh Almighty will dress you with the Dress of Majesty and Greatness and Wellness1

---

[40] Aḥmad, al-Musnad.

[41] Water closet: toilet; bathroom; restroom.

O Lord! We are Your weak servants. Send us who will teach us these things for the honor of Your Beloved ﷺ.

Bi hurmati 'l-Fātiḥah.

The Reality of 'Reforms'

May our day be blessed. These words we speak are the words that our Prophet ﷺ and *Awlīyā* make us say, leave aside what Allāh makes us say. What He ﷻ says is for the prophets and saints, it belongs to them. For us and people like us, these simple things that we learn benefit us.

Who teaches us these are *mu'allim*, teachers. What is wrong with saying *'mu'allim'* or *'hoja'*? Why do you corrupt your language? I curse them, saying, "May you not be able to speak at all!" They say, "Teacher, student, teacher." What do they say for *maktab*? *"Okul,"* school. We have never heard of the word *okul*, school here.

Here, take the reform in which the government said, "Give us your gold, it is old and take paper, it is new." Is there anyone who accepts this? No one accepts! "But you want reform, so then give us the gold." Now they took the gold from the people and gave them the new thing, paper! What is written on it? 5 *Liras*, 10 *Liras*, 100 *Liras*, 200 *Liras*. If you throw it into water, it melts. If you throw it into fire, it burns. If you tear it, it is gone. "You want reform, here! Take this, it is new."

All the governments went bankrupt, because each one of them has a paper in their hands that says on it, "This much, that much." Why do you cheat the people? Why do you cheat them? This man worked for you the whole day, was it for this piece of paper? "But this is reform!" May you sink with your reform, Arabs, Turks or whoever does this! Allāh Almighty will make them go down. They say "economy," *iqtisad*, and economy finished all of them, made them zero!

For forty years, Sulṭān Abdul Hamid ruled the Great State which was seven-million square kilometers. Everyone had golden coins or silver *majidiya* in their hands, but now they collected them all and put them in a safe. With what right did you collect them? Gold cannot be replaced with paper! They cheated the people with the numbers on it and now they say "unsolvable economic problems," I quote their expression. Now they hit the zero level. All of them shout in the streets: Europeans, Americans, all of them shout and scream, "We are hungry! We are thirsty!"

You can be left hungry or thirsty, but not without alcohol. They made you drunk, and you don't say, *"Bismillāhi 'r-Raḥmāni 'r-Raḥīm."* Okay, don't say it and find a way out of it if you can! They can't solve it without the *Bismillāh*, even in a thousand years. You can go up a mountain by climbing, but a man who fell into a well can't get out of it by climbing and rocks fall on his head while he is trying to get out and he gets stuck in it and he dies there.

What Happened to the Gold and Silver?

Accept the Truth, O small men! Use your minds, believe in what Allāh ﷻ sent! Value what Allāh ﷻ valued! Gold and silver is His ﷻ value and it was the value since life on Earth started, but after World War I the governments printed paper currency. If the governments print, can the people not print also (counterfeit)? They can, they print and put on the market and now no one knows if what he has in his hand is real or not. Will he go to a bank and have it validated each time? They messed it up and now their hands are in their pockets; they are all broke. They keep going back and forth, but all in vain. *Allāh, Allāh!*

وَأَن لَّيْسَ لِلْإِنسَانِ إِلَّا مَا سَعَىٰ

That man can have nothing but what he strives for.[42]

Man has nothing else other than what he does, but there is no work done anymore, they want money for free (welfare). They want only to enjoy and they sink into their pleasures. Floods took away their pleasures, snows fell on them, tornadoes made them upside-down, volcanoes, icebergs... Allāh! May Allāh forgive us! Say, "*Bismillāhi 'r-Raḥmāni 'r-Raḥīm*" so that you can be saved and if you don't say it, you will keep going down. You will go down!

Here they are all going down, like Abu Jahl, who called out, "Save me!" but no rope or chains could reach him and he got stuck in it. He said, "Call that one (Prophet) and I will take his hand and he can take me out." And the Prophet ﷺ did take him out. Allāh can take you out of these crises, but if you don't accept Allāh, you can't be saved and Allāh will degrade you. *Allāh! Amān, yā Rabbī*, don't degrade us! He ﷻ says, "I won't if you call

[42] Sūrat an-Najm, 53:39.

to Me: keep My order and I will give you your provision, I won't leave you hungry."

إِنَّ اللَّهَ هُوَ الرَّزَّاقُ ذُو الْقُوَّةِ الْمَتِينُ

Verily, Allāh is the Provider and Firm Possessor of Strength.[43]

He ﷻ says, "I am the All-Provider. I don't even leave an ant, I give their provisions, also. There are creatures that are smaller than them and I give their provisions, also."

O our Lord, forgive us! May You send us from Your Holy Servants who will show us the right ways.

We've all become bewildered ones. If you forget the *Bismillāh*, you forget Allāh and who forgets Allāh has no value. *Tawbah yā Rabbī, tawbah yā Rabbī, tawbah astaghfirullāh.* We may say, *"Bismillāhi 'r-Raḥmāni 'r-Raḥīm."* How beautiful!

With democracy or whatever it is, this one gets off and the other one gets on. Unless you change this, unless you remove the paper and bring gold, you can't straighten things. Everything has become a complete mess and they are stuck in it. *Tawbah yā Rabbī.*

As-salāmu 'alaykum. Jumu'ah Mubarak. May Allāh grant us strength and health for the honor of the Prophet ﷺ. There are *Awlīyā*, they give strength, then there is no need to go all the way up!

Fātiḥah.

ജ ഇ

[43] Sūrat az-Zariyat, 51:58.

Give Everyone Their Due Rights

We have entered the days when Sayyīdinā al-Mahdi ☼ will soon rule. Then, it will not be possible to deprive the Muslim of his rights and who does will be taken away to the Hereafter. Everyone will appreciate other's rights and will be thankful to their Lord and praise their Prophet ﷺ! *Fātiḥah*.

Therefore, who has a right, it will be his due right; it will not be taken back. *Haqqun*, there are rights due to their owners and conditions cannot be corrected until Judgement Day.

قال رسول الله صلى الله عليه وسلم, إن الله قد أعطى كل ذي حق حقه

Rasūlullāh ﷺ said, "Verily Allāh has given to each his right."[44]

For those who took the rights of kings, Allāh ﷻ will beat them to the point that they cannot button their shirts! Let them give back the rights to the king and their situation will be corrected; otherwise, up to Judgement Day there will be no improvement. Allāh's ﷻ orders are firm judgements from The Owner of Judgements!

This is an advice: if people do not give back the rights to kings (whom they deposed), nothing will be corrected. In Egypt, even if they brought and changed a hundred leaders, it is not possible for them to succeed, it would only be a struggle and revolution like the past one. This is a servant and that is a servant. If one servant is victorious over another, still his ego is like the other. A servant can never meet the leadership of kings!

These people are servants, they were honored with abundance through the presence of kings, but they rejected them and Allāh ﷻ kicked them out and threw them away from His Divine Door! These (current) ones are kicked out, because they do not keep the rights of the servants! The rights of the servants are important. Give them their rights, because if they are not given their rights, until Judgement Day that person will dwell in Hell forever! *Na'ūdhu billāh!*

---

[44] Ibn Majah; Aḥmad.

Let the people of Egypt understand, and if they do not understand, the whip will not be lifted from them. The whip is nothing, but a sword will also come. The sword will not be lifted from them until they return the rights to kings. *Tawbah, yā Rabbī! Tawbah, astaghfirullāh. Fātiḥah.*

The treasury of Egypt was equivalent to seven countries' treasuries. These Shayṭāns that kicked out the king, they destroyed the country. May Allāh ﷻ punish them! And people are ignorant, they are not following the Holy Shariʿah and blame and responsibility will be on them on Judgement Day and Allāh ﷻ will be angry with them! Give back rights to whom they are due. If you do not give it back, you will never succeed in this world or in the Hereafter!

Ya Sahib al-Imdad, Send Us Your Help!

As-salāmu ʿalaykum, ayyuha ʾl-hādirūn! It is said, *"As-salām qabl al-kalām, salām* is the first to be spoken." *As-salāmu ʿalaykum,* may Allāh's Peace be upon you, *wa raḥmatullāhi wa barakātuh,* and may His Mercy and Blessings be upon you. We may say, *"Bismillāhi ʾr-Raḥmāni ʾr-Raḥīm. Lā ilāha illa-Llāh Muḥammadun Rasūlullāh."* Who says this is dressed with the dress of honor and he becomes an honored one, whoever says, *"Lā ilāha illa-Llāh Sayyīdinā Muḥammadun Rasūlullāh."* I want to stand up to show my respect to his holy name a hundred or even a thousand times, but according to our situation we can only do this much and we want more!

وَقُل رَّبِّ زِدْنِي عِلْمًا

And say, "My Lord! Give me more knowledge."[45]

Rabbī zidnī ʿilman, My Lord, increase me in knowledge! The key to His Treasures is *Bismillāhi ʾr-Raḥmāni ʾr-Raḥīm.* We may stand up! There is real no treasure in this world because everything in *dunyā* is in *zawal* (demise).

Madad, yā RijālAllāh, O sincere servants of Allāh! May you send us heavenly support. *Yā Madad! Madad! Madad!* Ask for it, ask for *madad* as it comes down from Heavens and reaches you when you say, *"Bismillāhi ʾr-Raḥmāni ʾr-Raḥīm,"* the support of Heavens reaches you but it is a shame to ask *madad* for the goods of *dunyā,* it is a big shame!

For what should you ask *madad? Madad, yā Rabbī! Madad, yā Habībullāh! Madad, yā RijālAllāh!* Send us heavenly support that will give us strength in the way of Allāh's pleasure and acceptance. Our aim is the acceptance of our Lord Who created us and we don't seek or ask *madad* for anything else as it is a shame.

When you open your hands.... *Madad! Madad! Madad! Madad! Madad! Madad, yā Ṣāḥib al-Imdād,* O Master of Help! *Allāhu Akbar!* Help us! Send us Your *imdād* (help), *imdād Allāhi. Allāhu Akbar! Allāhu Akbar! Allāhu Akbar wa lillāhi ʾl-ḥamd!*

---

[45] Sūrah Taha, 20:114.

We should ask for *madad*, but not for what is in *dunyā*; *pttu* (spit) on *dunyā*, because a person who opens and raises his hands to Heavens to ask something for *dunyā* has no value. What is the value of *dunyā*?

الدني جيفة و طلابها كلابها

The world is a carcass and those who seek it out are dogs.[46]

Dunyā is a carcass and it is an unclean thing. Therefore, who raises his hands and asks for it has no honor, no mind, no religion, no faith, no *adab*! When you open your hands to ask *madad* from *Rabbu 'l-'Izza*, look for the one who is *Ṣāḥib al-Imdād*. The heavenly help comes to His Prophet ﷺ and from His Prophet it comes to the *walī* who is *Ṣāḥib al-Imdād*, the *Ṣāḥib at-Tasarruf* (who has authority to act). Direct yourself to him and say, "*Yā Ṣāḥib al-Imdād*! O Holy One Who sends help!" and don't ever ask anything for *dunyā* or your level will go down, because *dunyā* has no value!

Bismillāhi 'r-Raḥmāni 'r-Raḥīm! Here, this is the *adab*: the *Bismillāh*. A person who opens his hands to ask for the goods of *dunyā* must be ashamed, to say, "O Lord! Give me this, give me that," as it is beyond *adab*. This man doesn't know what he is asking; he doesn't ask for the precious stones, but he asks for rocks, he asks for pebbles! What will we do with pebbles? Ask for precious stones! Ask for precious stones! We ask for help. For what? Because there is the dirty ego that is inflicted upon us and there is Shayṭān from its kind. May his evil be far away from us! We seek refuge with Allāh from his evil.

When are we granted help? When we say, "*Bismillāhi 'r-Raḥmāni 'r-Raḥīm*." Even if there are *shayṭāns* as many as the number of people on Earth, one *Bismillāh* can burn them up and they can't harm you! *Yā Ṣāḥib al-Imdād*, O that holy one who sends help! He looks at the request for which that one is asking help. *Madad! Madad, yā RijālAllāh*! Going all the way to the Prophet ﷺ is not for us; we look to the one who is closest to us and there is the holy one who is filled with *imdād*, who receives the load of heavenly power. There are such holy ones, so ask from them, but ask for what? For nearness to Allāh Almighty! What you should ask is for nearness to Allāh Almighty! You cannot immediately go to the Sulṭān, as there is one who

---

[46] Al-Ajluni, Kashfu 'l-Khafa, Vol.1, p. 492; Kanzu 'l-Ummal, 8564.

represents Him: the power representing Allāh Almighty in the whole Creation is with His Prophet ﷺ, it is with our Master, the Master of Creation, Sayyīdinā Muḥammad al-Mustafa ﷺ! It is with him.

Ṣāḥib al-Imdād, the heavenly *madad* goes to Heavens and Earths through our Prophet ﷺ; therefore, when you say, *"Ṣāḥib al-Imdād!" ʿalā marātibihim,* you can't address the Prophet ﷺ so suddenly. There are holy ones who have reached nearness to him ﷺ who are filled with the *barakah* of our Prophet ﷺ, so look for them, search!

فاسْأَلْ بِهِ خَبِيرًا

Ask (from) who is expert.[47]

Allāh ﷻ is saying, "Ask the one who has the knowledge of the secret matter," as not just anyone can do it. Look for that one who has the power that if he kicks this Earth, he can pull it out of its orbit and throw it away! He may look like a speck, but his magnificence, the power that is with that one who is the *Ṣāḥib al-Imdād* can pull the Earth from its orbit and throw it away as they have such a power.

O *Ṣāḥib al-Imdād,* reach! We are left helpless. *Lā hadd wa lā yanhadd.* There are holy ones who are ready in service, the honored ones:

وَلَقَدْ كَرَّمْنَا بَنِي آدَمَ

We have honored the Children of Adam.[48]

"For the honor of My Glory, I granted Man such a rank that I granted its secret to the ones who can carry as much as I tell them." Man is *Hazrat al-Insān.* Allāh *Dhu 'l-Jalāl* honored him with divine honoring, but today, ignorant ones and tyrants made all the people zero; they don't appreciate their value and are crushing them. *Hāsha*! Those whom Allāh ﷻ glorified, elevated and said, "My *Khalif,*" for him:

إنِّي جَاعِلٌ فِي الأَرْضِ خَلِيفَة

Verily, I am making a deputy on Earth.[49]

---

[47] Sūrat al-Furqān, 25:59.

[48] Sūrat al-'Isrā, 17:70.

How to Summon Sahib al-Imdad and Remove Evil

Allāh ﷻ said, "Adam and his generations are My *Khalifah* on Earth." Who leaves this and makes insults is together with Shayṭān and he loses his attribute as a human being and finally takes the ugly form of Shayṭān. They have tails and Shayṭān also has a tail, and his appearance is very ugly. Whoever you see is an ugly one, so know that he is from the followers of Shayṭān and leave that place! To be saved from it, say, "*Yā Ṣāḥib al-Imdād*! Help! Reach to help us!" There is the holy one who is *Ṣāḥib al-Imdād,* who reaches and says, "Say quickly, '*Bismillāhi 'r-Raḥmāni 'r-Raḥīm*!' Say it so I may reach you, because if you don't say it, I don't reach. Say, '*Bismillāhi 'r-Raḥmāni 'r-Raḥīm*! O our Lord! May You not deprive us of the blessings of the *Bismillāh*!' and our Lord dresses us with the honorable dress of servanthood with the blessing of *Bismillāhi 'r-Raḥmāni 'r-Raḥīm.*"

Look at the face of the one who says the *Bismillāh*; there is *nūr* in his face and the face of who doesn't say it is all dark. We may also say, "*Bismillāhi 'r-Raḥmāni 'r-Raḥīm.*" How beautiful! "*Bismillāhi 'r-Raḥmāni 'r-Raḥīm*! *Bismillāhi 'Lladhī lā yadurru ma'a 'smihi shay'un fi 'l-'arḍi wa lā fi 's-samā'i wa Huwa 's-Sami'u 'l-'Alīm.*" Read this and blow on yourself and every evil will go away from you. *Allāhu Akbar! Allāhu Akbar! Allāhu Akbar wa lillāhi 'l-ḥamd*!

How beautiful is the *Bismillāh*! *Bismillāhi 'r-Raḥmāni 'r-Raḥīm* gives life, gives honor, gives power, gives glory, gives familiarity. Continue its *dhikr*; make its *dhikr* separately every day, reciting it daily starting from seven times, then forty, then seventy and one-hundred times. Say the *Bismillāh,* and this is for the common people; for those who are beyond them, there is permission to recite the *Bismillāh* according to their service. Recite it and don't fear!

Say, "*Bismillāhi 'r-Raḥmāni 'r-Raḥīm*" and all doors will open! There is no door that the *Bismillāh* cannot open, but you should know what to ask for; if you ask for a carcass, it is a shame on you. "This one who asks for a carcass, expel him from the door! Throw him so he struggles among the carcasses!" What does the one who knows ask? "*Yā Ṣāḥib al-Imdād*! May You protect us from the hands of the dirty ego, dirty Shayṭān. O Lord! May we

---

[49] Sūrat al-Baqara, 2:30.

walk with Your servanthood, *yā Rabbī*! You created us for Your servanthood, so may we be aware of it and make Your service." Then we may say, "*Bismillāhi 'r-Raḥmāni 'r-Raḥīm, Bismillāhi 'r-Raḥmāni 'r-Raḥīm, Bismillāhi 'r-Raḥmāni 'r-Raḥīm*!" Now look and see, are there any doors that will not open? Don't do it with the intention, "Let me experience it." It is not with experience; rather, it requires faith, what the Children of Adam need is faith. You should believe, because if you don't believe you have no value, you are trash, you have no good, there is no beauty in your face, your face cannot be looked upon as you are a wild one and the honor of humanity is taken off you. Be a human being, but for what? To make service for your Lord!

Allāh is asking, "Why did I create Man?"

وَمَا خَلَقْتُ الْجِنَّ وَالْإِنسَ إِلَّا لِيَعْبُدُونِ

I have only created jinn and human beings so that they may worship Me.[50]

Rabbu 'l-'Izza ﷻ is saying, "I created human beings and *jinn* to worship Me, that I am the Creator of Earths and Heavens, *Mulk and Malakūt*," which have no boundaries, and there is also the world of *Jabarūt* where *Mulk* and *Malakūt* are not even a speck in comparison! One trembles, one trembles!

The Real Attributes Men and Women

O small men! You cannot be Man by wearing fashionable clothes, but only with *adab*. Don't follow fashion, you will become ugly! Ladies have *jamāl*, beauty, and men have *kamāl*, perfection. Open your hands and say, "*Bismillāhi 'r-Raḥmāni 'r-Raḥīm*," and Allāh ﷻ will dress ladies from His *Jamāl* Attribute and men from His *Kamāl* Attribute. How beautiful, how beautiful! They have no troubles, no sorrows, no hardness.

"*Yā Ṣāḥib al-Imdād*!" Call him and say, "Reach us!" and he will reach. He saves you from filth and from sorrows also, he saves you from the humiliation of *dunyā*, from the torment of *Akhirah*. Allāh Almighty grants you such a rank that there is no one who can know its boundaries other than our Prophet ﷺ. Show respect for our Prophet ﷺ, Haḍrati Muḥammad al-Mustafa ﷺ, the Master of the Creation!

---

[50] Sūrat adh-Dhariyat, 51:56-57.

كَلَّا لَا تُطِعْهُ وَاسْجُدْ وَاقْتَرِبْ

Prostrate and draw near to Allāh.[51]

Allāh is saying, "Make *sajda* and draw near." *Allāhu Akbar*! Say, "*Bismillāhi 'r-Raḥmāni 'r-Raḥīm,*" and draw near. The ones without the *Bismillāh* are not allowed to draw near, because those without the *Bismillāh* are unclean, because they allow their ego to come in between. So they are dirty and unclean:

إِنَّمَا الْمُشْرِكُونَ نَجَسٌ فَلاَ يَقْرَبُواْ الْمَسْجِدَ الْحَرَامَ بَعْدَ عَامِهِمْ هَـذَا

Truly, the polytheists are impure, so let them not approach al-Masjid al-Haram after this, their (final) year.[52]

Is it not so? Allāh Almighty prohibited it in this holy verse that descended to our Prophet ﷺ, saying, "Impure ones should not enter *Baytu 'l-Mu'azzam* after this year as they are *najasun*, impure."

If you want to be clean and pure, say, "*Bismillāhi 'r-Raḥmāni 'r-Raḥīm.*" If you put cologne or perfumes on your hands, face or other places, if you say, "Let me look beautiful and smell nice," still you stink! *Mushriks* (polytheists) have such a bad smell that when they are buried, even the vicinity of their graves stink because they used other things in *dunyā* to look beautiful and didn't seek from their Lord the beauty of *Bismillāhi 'r-Raḥmāni 'r-Raḥīm*. Then whoever visits their grave runs away!

When they bury you one day, may you find your grave as a garden of roses of *Bismillāh*. Don't forget the *Bismillāh*, O Sulṭāns! O Sulṭāns! O those who think of themselves highly, who say, "We are this, we are that!" When you die in such a way, you who are without the *Bismillāh,* you are tyrants and the followers of Shayṭān, the cruel ones, the bad ones, the smelly ones! If their reality appeared, the whole world would run away from them. Don't look to the dress you wear, but wear your spiritual dress:

بسم الله الرحمن الرحيم , بسم الله الذي لا يضر مع اسمه شيء في الأرض
ولا في السماء وهو السميع العليم

---

[51] Sūrat al-'Alaq, 96:19.

[52] Sūrat at-Tawbah, 9:28.

In the Name of Allāh, with whose Name nothing on Earth or in the sky can harm and He is The All-Hearing and All-Knowing.[53]

When you say, "*Yā Ṣāḥib al-Imdād,*" recite the *Bismillāh*. Whenever you ask for help say the *Bismillāh,* because with Allāh's Name everything is completed. How beautiful is this *Bismillāh*! What an honor it is for us! O Lord! Don't deprive us of its honor, that we may always say, "*Bismillāhi 'r-Raḥmāni 'r-Raḥīm.*" Then weapons and cannons fired at them will turn back on their enemy and fall on their heads! Don't fear! Cannons are not the power, the real power is in the one who can say, "*Bismillāhi 'r-Raḥmāni 'r-Raḥīm,*" whom, if he kicks the Earth he can pull it out of its orbit and throw it away! There are men who are small like the size of a finger.

O Lord! May He ﷻ dress us from the virtues of the *Bismillāh*. It is not for us to ask this directly from our Lord, so we call the *Ṣāḥib al-Imdād*. Call him each time you are in a difficulty and say, "*Yā Ṣāḥib al-Imdād*! *Bismillāhi 'r-Raḥmāni 'r-Raḥīm.*" Don't fear, don't fear! If he goes to Hellfire he can extinguish it, let alone the toys of this *dunyā*! He can walk on water.

The Sultan's Ring and the Dervish

Once upon a time, a dervish embarked on a ship and was traveling the sea with other passengers. After a while there were some noises, screams and shouting. "What happened?" they asked.

Someone answered, "The ring of the sulṭān who is traveling in this ship was stolen."

The dervish said, "Astonishing, and what will they do?"

"Well, they will search everyone inside the ship and whoever stole it will be thrown in the water."

They searched everyone in the ship and this one was a poor dervish. They also came to him and said, "We will search you also, O holy one."

The poor dervish! He was deeply offended and said, "Okay, wait for a minute."

---

[53] (Sunan Ibn Majah, Book 34, Hadith 3869)

They waited and he stood up and went to the railing of the ship, said, *"Bismillāhi 'r-Raḥmāni 'r-Raḥīm"* and jumped overboard, then he walked over the waves, saying, *Bismillāhi 'r-Raḥmāni 'r-Raḥīm."*

Seeing this, the people were ashamed and said, "How could we do this to such a holy person? How did we lose him?"

He just left; the sea carried him, because he said, *"Bismillāhi 'r-Raḥmāni 'r-Raḥīm! Bismillāhi 'r-Raḥmāni 'r-Raḥīm!"*

Sayyidina Hasan al-Basri

Hasan al-Basri ق is from the great scholars, and I think he is also from the early *Tabi'in*. He resided in Baghdad, where the big, holy Dijla River runs through. Who wants to cross it gets on a raft and they sail to the other side. One day, Hasan al-Basri ق came to cross the river and he waited for the raft while sitting on a rock. After a while, all of a sudden Ḥabību 'l-'Ajami ق showed up, a holy one who is a non-Arab.

He said, *"As-salāmu 'alaykum,* O scholar of the nation! What are you waiting for?"

Hasan al-Basri ق said, "I am waiting for the raft to cross to the other side."

He said, "Astonishing! Why should a person like you have to wait for the raft? Look, I will cross it." He simply said, *"Bismillāhi 'r-Raḥmāni 'r-Raḥīm"* and crossed the river walking on the water, then he said, "Is it suitable for a man like you to wait for the raft?"

By saying, *"Bismillāhi 'r-Raḥmāni 'r-Raḥīm, Bismillāhi 'r-Raḥmāni 'r-Raḥīm, Bismillāhi 'r-Raḥmāni 'r-Raḥīm,"* he crossed the river in three steps! There is no end to the miracles of the *Bismillāh*. O son! Keep the *Bismillāh* and don't fear as you can destroy. The *Ṣāḥib al-Waqt* will destroy unbelief with the *Bismillāh*.

Amān yā Rabbī! May You look upon us to convict our egos.

Don't quit reciting one-hundred times daily, *"Bismillāhi 'r-Raḥmāni 'r-Raḥīm."* Don't fear, don't fear! You can destroy enemies from a distance.

O our Lord! May You not deprive us of the power and the honor of the *Bismillāh*. But before addressing our Lord, we say, *"Yā Ṣāḥib al-Imdad*, who is the Owner of *Madad* and where is his *tasarruf?"* In *Bismillāhi 'r-Raḥmāni 'r-Raḥīm*!

May Allāh make your faces enlightened and your hearts pure; may your station be the station of honor in *dunyā* and may your station be Paradise and watching the Beauty of Allāh ﷻ in *Akhirah*! Be happy that they are listening to these few words. My prayers are with those who listen. You also pray for me, pray for me.

Allāhu Akbar! Allāhu Akbar! Allāhu Akbar wa lillāhi 'l-ḥamd. Allāh bless you!

$$سَلَامٌ قَوْلًا مِن رَّبٍّ رَّحِيم$$

(For them) the word from a Merciful Lord is "Peace!"[54]

Don't forget me in your prayers, make *du'a* for me. My goal is to overcome this unbelief, not to stay longer in this *dunyā*; it is to put this unbelief under my feet, to convict my dirty ego. Be lions! Be lions! *Inshā'Allāh* we will be honored with the service of Mahdi ؏ and Isa ؏!

As-salāmu 'alaykum!

৪৩ ৎ৪

---

[54] Sūrat YaSīn, 36:58.

A Good Life Here and Hereafter

Bismillāhi 'r-Raḥmāni 'r-Raḥīm.* We may say the *Ismu 'l-Jalīl* of our Lord, *"Lā ilāha illa-Llāh Sayyīdinā Muḥammadun Rasūlullāh."* It is said *yawmun jadīd, rizqun jadīd,* "A new day, a new provision." Allāh Almighty sustains His Divine Grants in the apparent, too. *A'ūdhu billāhi min ash-shayṭāni 'r-rajīm.* Why does He ﷻ make us recite the *"a'ūdhu"*?

فاسْتَعِذْ بِاللّهِ مِنَ الشَّيْطَانِ الرَّجِيم

Seek refuge with Allāh from Shayṭān, the Accursed.[55]

Dastūr, yā RijālAllāh! May there be a heavenly support from the holy ones that we say a few words and open *inshā'Allāh.* Our first word is, *"Bismillāhi 'r-Raḥmāni 'r-Raḥīm."* The *Bismillāh* should be our first word (as it means). "The *Bismillāh* is Your Pure Name and who remembers it is purified. Who says 'Allāh' can reach everything he desires." What a beautiful teaching! It teaches people that any act without the *Bismillāh* is cut off, as the Prophet ﷺ said:

كل عمل لم يبدأ باسم الله فهو أبتر

Any 'amal which does not begin with 'Bismillāhi 'r-Raḥmāni 'r-Raḥīm' is cut off; it has no continuity.[56]

This is the Word of Allāh ﷻ and the teaching of the Prophet ﷺ. Whichever act starts without the *Bismillāh* it is cut off, it has no result. *Yawm al-jadīd, rizq al-jadīd!* In every new day there are the grants of Allāh Almighty for His servants, His blessings and His gifts for them. Allāh Almighty, *Jalla Jalāluhu*!

O People, listen! You are human beings; therefore, you should listen and understand for what purpose does Allāh Almighty make us recite the *Bismillāh*? For our every deed to succeed. The key for opening all difficulties is *"Bismillāhi 'r-Raḥmāni 'r-Raḥīm"*. Allāh Almighty wants His servant's lives to be sweet. Whoever wants every day and every hour of this life to be

---

[55] Sūrat an-Nahl, 16:98.

[56] Aḥmad, *Musnad.*

sweet, whoever wants a life without troubles, sorrows, hardness, Allāh Almighty says:

لا يُرِيدُ بِكُمُ الْعُسْرَ

Allāh intends for you ease and does not intend for you hardship.[57]

Allāh Almighty says, "I did not give you a life that will be a burden to you and I never want to put a burden on you. I don't want My servant to be crushed, I don't want him to live in difficulties. *Lā yurīdu bikumu 'l-'usrā,* an easy and sweet life, this is what I want. I did not create My servants to be crushed in *dunyā,* instead they should enjoy the *dunyā.*" How should they enjoy? "I want them to spend a comfortable life full of pleasures, this is My desire. I created My servant and sent him to *dunyā,* not to crush him there."

Rabbu 'l 'Izza, our Lord, Allāh Almighty says, "I did not order anything to make hardship for you. Everything should go so easy for you and your day should be a sweet day. It should not be a bitter life for you, not a life of poison. I want you to live comfortably and happily in *dunyā,* in contentment, being busy with My servanthood; but you followed the evil Shayṭān who wants to cast on you the burdens of *dunyā,* so that your *dunyā* life will be like poison!"

Allāh Almighty wants a beautiful life for His servants and to the contrary, Shayṭān wants to corrupt the beautiful life Allāh Almighty taught Mankind. His whole hatred and struggle is for human beings not to find comfort, for them to live in misery and their *dunyā* life to be as the wheat crushed between two millstones! Shayṭān wants our life to be poisonous and in hardship. Therefore, to open our day, for the door of a comfortable life to open for us, human beings should first say, "*Bismillāhi 'r-Raḥmāni 'r-Raḥīm.*" Say the *Bismillāh*!

اذْكُرُونِي أَذْكُرْكُمْ وَاشْكُرُوا لِي وَلا تَكْفُرُونَ

Remember Me, I will remember you. Give thanks to Me
and do not be ungrateful towards Me.[58]

---

[57] Surat al-Baqara, 2:185.
[58] Sūrat al-Baqara, 2:152.

Fadhkurūnī adhkurkum, "Remember My *Ismu 'l-Jalīl* and I will grant to you a life filled with My blessings!" *W 'ashkurū lī,* "Be grateful to Me." *Wa lā takfurūn,* "And don't deny Me as it is a shame for you!" This is the address. "O Man! I created you, I made everything ready for you on Earth so that you won't have any hardship. This is the situation, but you don't accept this, you don't appreciate this and you fall into one hardship after another, like the wheat crushed between two millstones. I don't want this! I sent you to *dunyā,* I didn't send you to be crushed between two millstones! It is only a temporary life so acknowledge Me and everything will be beautiful for you! I like good deeds, I like beautiful servants and their beautiful deeds. If you want this, start saying My *Ismu 'l-Jalīl, 'Bismillāhi 'r-Raḥmāni 'r-Raḥīm,'* and your every doing will go easy; it will flow like water, there will be no difficulty in front of you and your life will go easy and sweet."

This is because Allāh Almighty did not want any hardship for you; He presented you the most beautiful life, but what is its key? To say, "*Bismillāhi 'r-Raḥmāni 'r-Raḥīm*" and stand up for Allāh! What comes first, what are you granted when you stand up for Allāh? The sweet life. Allāh Almighty doesn't want for you a life like poison. *Hāsha! Hāsha thumma kallā.* He ﷻ didn't make it as a poison for Mankind, but He made it a sweet life, *hayāt at-ṭayyiba.* "Let them be My guests in this *dunyā* life and live comfortably. Let them be My guests and listen to Me, return to Me, and I will grant them everything."

The Reality of Public Protests

But human beings don't do this. What is the key for this? To say, "*Bismillāhi 'r-Raḥmāni 'r-Raḥīm*". Why do you run in the streets[59]? Now in all countries, the public streets have turned into streams of people who don't even know what they want. What is it that they want? *Hayāt at-ṭayyiba,* the sweet life, the nice life. But you are the guests of Allāh Almighty in *dunyā,* and does Allāh Almighty give a hardship to the ones who are His guests? No, He ﷻ doesn't, but foolish men are following Shayṭān and can't enjoy life as they fall from one trouble to another. Why do you men and women run in the streets? Did Allāh order you, "O People! Go out into the streets and scream!" This is not suitable for your humanity. What is suitable for your

---

[59] Protest marches.

humanity is for you to return to your Lord. When you don't accept Your Creator, then no one accepts you and Shayṭān makes you a toy in his hand. The streets are filled with people. What do they want, they don't know.

When the Muslim soldiers entered Izmir, there was a group of people from other religions who also called with the rest; Muslims said, "Long live!" and the others also called, "Long live!"

"Who should live long?" asked one.

They said, "Whoever won, may they live long!"

Look at who makes you win. Why do you run after Shayṭān? Shayṭān ridiculed you and made you run in the streets like wild animals, he makes you scream and swear. Now you have no rest or comfort and nothing to eat or drink. All their claim is protesting in the streets, which is not suitable for the *adab* of Mankind.

When Allāh Almighty appoints a servant to rule over you who is covered in black hair, even if the rest of him is all black obey him, because he also can protect you! Obey him, saying, "Allāh appointed him for us!" and take the attitude of *adab*, remain with *adab*. It means, "Allāh Almighty appointed for us this servant, so we may walk on his way and say, *'Bismillāhi 'r-Raḥmāni 'r-Raḥīm.' Yā Rabbī*! May You make this servant of Yours a mercy for us, not wrath."

They don't say this, but scream in the streets. Say one *"Bismillāh"* and you can destroy your obstacles and the doings of *shayṭāns*, but they don't say it. They proclaim, "We will never say it as we are socialist people; we are filthy ones, we belong to the wild level, those who run, scream and kick in the jungles! We don't want the level of those who go to the mosque." Okay then, take what is suitable for you! Run and shout all day, but you won't be well regarded. The world of *Malakūt*[60] does not respond to you, because you are out of the level that is protected; you entered the wild level of four-legged animals. If you were in the human level, you went to mosques. You have temples; go there and call, "O our Lord Who created us! May You grant us the *hayāt at-ṭayyiba*!"

---

[60] The Heavenly Realm.

"O My Servant! You are given the key to the beautiful life, *Bismillāhi 'r-Raḥmāni 'r-Raḥīm,* which opens for you all locked doors and all the treasures, and the doors of eight Paradises. Say, *'Bismillāhi 'r-Raḥmāni 'r-Raḥīm!'*"

But they will never say this, so the angels reply, "You are that arrogant? Okay, run in the streets and may you not find what you seek."

O human beings who have become animals who deny their Lord! You scream in the streets? Who will answer you? Who has ever received an answer like this anyway? You are humans, so prove your humanity by calling out, "O our Lord! *Bi 'smika 'l-'Azhīm,* we seek refuge in Your Holy Name, *al-'Azīm.* Save us, O Lord! May You send Your beautiful, powerful servants who will teach us our humanity. May You send us the deputies of prophets who will save us from being animals and we will follow them."

What business do you have in the streets? For whom are the mosques? Do dogs ever enter a mosque? Neither a dog nor anyone from the wild level enters there. Don't sleep! Open your eyes so that you know the magnificence of humanity and what a beautiful life Allāh Almighty appointed for His servants! But they kick it away and they gather behind Shayṭān and run. Who makes them go out and shout in the streets, who makes people uneasy, who makes them kill each other, who crushes them in fights and wars? Shayṭān.

Allāh Almighty says, "I appointed *hayāt at-ṭayyiba,* a beautiful life for you. Start with the *Bismillāh,* turn towards Me and I will make every day a beautiful day to go nicely and you will never face any troubles. Turn to Me!"

"No, we will scream and protest, no matter what!"

Okay, scream, but you can't find a place that will answer your call. You are running and screaming in the streets. Who are you running to, why are you screaming, what do you seek and from whom, what is it that you want? They don't know. Shayṭān pulled them out of the human level and made them enter the four-legged wild ones' level and said, "Run! Don't look at the mosque, look at the streets!"

If they say one *Bismillāh,* Allāh Almighty will make *dunyā* change; this *dunyā* becomes a different *dunyā* for Allāh's servants who say His *Ismu 'l-Jalīl.*

يَوْمَ تُبَدَّلُ الأَرْضُ غَيْرَ الأَرْضِ وَالسَّمَاوَاتُ وَبَرَزُوا لِلّهِ الْوَاحِدِ الْقَهَّارِ

On the Day when the Earth will be changed to another Earth and so will be the Heavens, and (men) will be marshalled forth before Allāh, The One, The Irresistible.[61]

On that day, Allāh Almighty changes *dunyā* to another *dunyā*; He ﷻ appoints a nice life, a sweet life for you where you don't feel hunger, thirst or exhaustion. But now that wildness is everywhere, because Shayṭān whips them, "Scream, shout!" You can't gain anything by screaming and shouting. Say, "O Allāh! For the honor of Your Beloved, may You appoint over us the servants You love so that our works straighten and our provision becomes plenty."

As long as you don't say *"Bismillāhi 'r-Raḥmāni 'r-Raḥīm"*, your provision will be insufficient, even the whole *dunyā* will be insufficient for you! Even if you save treasures still you will not be satisfied, and you will stay in hardship and you will not be saved. O Mankind! If you want to be saved from hardships, say the Magnificent Name of Who created you: *Bismillāhi 'r-Raḥmāni 'r-Raḥīm*, in the Name of Allāh, Who is *ar-Raḥmān* and *ar-Rahīm*, The Most Beneficent, The Most Merciful! Recite it even in this form and your life will improve!

O Lord! Forgive us. We are left without a master! Send us a sulṭān so that when we look at his face we tremble! A sulṭān should not be like yourselves. Our Lord will send such a sulṭān. *Bismillāhi 'r-Raḥmāni 'r-Raḥīm.* O our Lord! May You give health to our bodies, give joy to our thoughts and mind. May You grant *nūr* to our hearts, *barakah* to our every work. May our life and death be clean, may we come up to Your Divine Presence clean.

Bismillāhi 'r-Raḥmāni 'r-Raḥīm. When the Angel of Death comes to take your soul, he will say, *"Bismillāhi 'r-Raḥmāni 'r-Raḥīm"* and take it. One day the Angel of Death will come and your soul will leave your body and by him saying, *"Bismillāhi 'r-Raḥmāni 'r-Raḥīm,"* your exit from *dunyā* will be in such a comfortable way, in a wonderful state that is impossible to define! The people who sink into *dunyā* and became pressed, their souls are taken by force, by pulling and hurting. Then it will be too late for them, as they didn't say the *Bismillāh*.

---

[61] Sūrat Ibrahim, 14:48.

O our Lord! May You make us from those who don't forget the *Bismillāh*! May we say Your *Ismu 'l-Jalīl* and our troubles go away, the hardness in us may go away. O Lord! May You dress on us from the treasures that are in the *Ka'bah*, the dress of faith, the dress of Islam, the dress of honor, the dress of joy, the dress of blessings, the dress of knowledge, the dress of softness, the dress of servanthood, the dress of familiarity! May You not make us from those who are squeezed and pressed in *dunyā*.

Bismillāhi 'r-Raḥmāni 'r-Raḥīm. Forgive us, *yā Rabbī*! Forgive us, *yā Rabbī*! We are left astonished. *Anta Rabbu 'l-Jalīl, Rabbu 'l-Jalīl*, there is no end to Your Magnificence! Forgive us, *yā Rabbī*! May You send us Your servants who will show us Your beautiful ways, *yā Rabbī*!

They said an asteroid is passing by the Earth and the whole world has been in a panic for two days. Why? A rock the size of a fist passes by and all people are in panic. Why should you panic? We say, "*Bi haqqi Bismillāhi 'r-Raḥmāni 'r-Raḥīm*, by the right of the *Bismillāh*. O stone! Don't come towards us, but turn back in the direction from which you came!"

If a *wali*, servant of Allāh says this, he can return and throw it to that side. Now all people are left bewildered, saying, "What will happen to us?" Accept Allāh and goodness will come to you! Accept His Prophet ﷺ, praise and love him, and your *dunyā* as well as your *Akhirah* will become prosperous. When he says, "*Bismillāhi 'r-Raḥmāni 'r-Raḥīm*! *Bi haqqi Bismillāhi 'r-Raḥmāni 'r-Raḥīm*, turn back in the direction from which you came!" it turns.

By the right of *Bismillāhi 'r-Raḥmāni 'r-Raḥīm*, O our Lord, may You grant us health and wellness from Your generous grants and grant us the power of faith! Make us far away from ugly acts and may we not become ugly.

Everyone wants to look beautiful. They put makeup and wear fashionable clothes, but beauty is not with these, beauty comes down from Heavens. Raise your hands to the Heavens and say, "*Yā Rabbī*! Make us beautiful. You are the Most Beautiful One! Send us a speck from the Ocean of Beauty so we may look beautiful to You, *yā Rabbī*!"

Some wives strive to look beautiful for the people outside their homes and drew away from humanity; they became disobedient to their Lord and are denied the beautiful life. Their appearance is human, but they have become *shayṭāns*; they turned into such a herd.

May Allāh forgive us! May He send us His holy servants who will show us the right way. *Yā Rabbī*! Forgive us.

Wa min Allāhi 't-tawfiq, bi hurmati 'l-Fātiḥah.

Always Try to Avoid Fighting

B*ismillāhi 'r-Raḥmāni 'r-Raḥīm.* My Arabic is little. Once upon a time, I was traveling with the Cypriot pilgrims. *SubḥānAllāh,* in those days we used to get a ride from Nicosia, Lefkosia, to Beirut, then from Beirut take a bus to *Shām* (Damascus), from where we walked to Hijāz (Muslim Holy Land in Saudi Arabia), or take what the Arabs call a "Pullman," a railcar.

We were traveling by car or bus, and we reached the border. There was tension between the people of *Shām* and the Jordanians, especially among the scholars with no mind, who used to insult the Jordanian government, the Hashemite Kingdom. Some scholars had no mind or manners and they used to insult the king. Therefore, police intelligence was stationed at the border for those entering from Jordan, especially heedless ones from the People of *Shām.* They used to question them and would even send them back from the border.

As I reached the border, I began to arrange some things to prepare ourselves for the trip. On the way to the border, *mashā'Allāh* I saw a very tall man.

He said to me, "O Shaykh!"

I said, "Yes."

"What do you think of this and that?"

I understood from him that the ones traveling to his country (from *Shām*) were against the *Ahlu 'l-Bayt* because of the Palestinians that were living in the west of *Shām,* so he tried to make me speak to see if I was against the king and, if so, then he would send me away directly.

After speaking continuously a long while, he said, "What do you think?"

I answered, "O brother, I do not understand Arabic, I am Turkish."

He said, "Why didn't you tell me before?" and became angry.

I said, "Why are you angry? I did not understand, my Arabic is little!"

"Little, but you do not understand!" he said.

I said, "I understood that much. I am Turkish. We are going from *Shām* to Hijāz."

So we managed the situation by saying, "My Arabic is little," and therefore, this was the way to safety and this set us free. They chained Amīr Hussayn and exiled him to Cyprus, where my father served him.

I will tell you a story. One shaykh who was very peculiar and funny. was the imam for Sharīf Hussayn, may Allāh ﷻ have mercy on his soul. He had a small shop where he manufactured and sold soap. The servants of Sharīf Hussayn came to visit and sit with him from outside the walls of his house in Nicosia.

One day when I was eight or ten years of age, as I was walking by I saw them sitting together. Some of his servants wore the traditional headdress, the *'iqal*. There were some children standing behind me, and. one of them said, "The servants of Shaykh Hussayn are sitting with black snakes on their heads." I saw that and began to run away because there was a snake on their heads! And like this, *SubḥānAllāhi 'l-'Aliyyu 'l-'Azhīm,* we were acquainted.

May Allāh forgive us and forgive our sins *inshā'Allāh.*

Prophet ﷺ said, "There will come a time for everyone to receive their due rights." More honor and sovereignty to the Children of the Prophet ﷺ as it must be; things must return to their origin. The Arabs have no respect left for the Children of the Prophet ﷺ. What gives them the right?

Fātiḥah.

Traps that Take Us Far from Allāh

Asbahnā wa asbaha 'l-mulku Lillāh wa nahnu 'abidan Lillāh. As-salāmu 'alaykum ayyuha 'l-hādirūn. What can we do? We got up with *khayr*, goodness, *inshā'Allāh.* Who awakens with *khayr* awakens with the consciousness of worshipping His Lord. What is the place of one who has no consciousness for worshipping His Lord? It is below the animals! Animals know what they should do and human beings who don't know what they should do are below the level of animals.

As-salāmu 'alaykum. Alḥamdulillāh. We should say the "*Bismillāh,*" as our strength is with it. Say, "*Bismillāhi 'r-Raḥmāni 'r-Raḥīm,*" and you will be strong, no one can stand against you. Even if the whole world was Shayṭān, it could not stand against *Bismillāhi 'r-Raḥmāni 'r-*Raḥīm, it will be crushed, melted and gone! *Bismillāhi 'r-Raḥmāni 'r-Raḥīm*! Is it not so? It walks over everything. The power in the *Bismillāh* can crush and walk over everything and who believes in this can defeat the whole world!

Bismillāhi 'r-Raḥmāni 'r-Raḥīm! O our Lord, I got up for Your worship! You are my Lord and I am in existence to worship You. Accept us, support us, O Lord! May You accept our worship O Lord! We are helpless and weak. May You strengthen us!

Our ego is pushing us with Shayṭān! Shayṭān says, "Come and be with me. Come and be with me!" When Shayṭān says this, what is its meaning? "Come and work for me. Come and be my animal!" He doesn't say this, but says, "Come and work for me and I will pay you." With what are you paid? With troubles and ugliness.

What is it that Shayṭān can pay people? He ties you up with troubles and when you try to solve one of them, he ties another knot; while you try to solve that, he ties another knot. This is his job! He multiplies one trouble into thousands and makes people fall into them. For this, he approaches and says, "Come to me. Is that the *adhān*? Let it be called and you continue to sleep as there is plenty of time." He makes you sleep and he throws a filthy quilt on top of you and says, "Here it is, sleep and be comfortable! Don't get up, sleep, sleep as there is plenty of time."

And the one who doesn't use his head and know his honor immediately says, "Of course, let me sleep a little bit more." He sleeps and forgets his worship, his servanthood and there is no worship left for him anymore. Whoever wakes up and says, *Aʿūdhu billāhi min ash-Shayṭāni 'r-rajīm. Bismillāhi 'r-Raḥmāni 'r-Raḥīm*, "O Lord, I seek refuge with You from Shayṭān and his invitation. Protect me O Lord!" Allāh says, "I will protect you, O My servant!" So say, *"Aʿūdhu billāhi min ash-Shayṭāni 'r-rajīm. Bismillāhi 'r-Raḥmāni 'r-Raḥīm."*

فَإِذَا قَرَأْتَ الْقُرْآنَ فَاسْتَعِذْ بِاللهِ مِنَ الشَّيْطَانِ الرَّجِيمِ .إِنَّهُ لَيْسَ لَهُ
سُلْطَانٌ عَلَى الَّذِينَ آمَنُوا وَعَلَى رَبِّهِمْ يَتَوَكَّلُونَ

Now whenever you read this Qur'ān, seek refuge with Allāh from Shayṭān, the Accursed. Behold, he has no power over those who have attained faith and who in their Sustainer place their trust.[62]

Allāh ﷻ says, "I am the One Who created you. I am the One Who is the Lord of the Earths and the Heavens. I am Who created them!"

What do you think, that they came out of nowhere, that this world and all these different kinds of creatures on it were made by themselves? Spit on what you study, as well as what you teach! Some tell me, "It is nature, Shaykh Effendi!" Does nature put you through the grinder, crush you, turn you into fertilizer and throw you away? You believe in the nature, but don't believe in Allāh. They say now there are different new names and expressions. "This is nature and we are following it." With this thinking, Mankind has become humiliated and lost their honor! They forgot The One Who brought them into existence from the nonexistence. *Yā Hū*! Did you come to existence by yourself? "My mother gave birth to us, so we exist." Really? So did your mother create you? Then Who created your mother, why don't you say? They cannot say, "There is Allāh, The Master of the Creation." Shayṭān says, "I have no owner, I exist on my own."

The cursed ones, Shayṭān and those who believe in him, are teaching what Shayṭān says! Ever since life on Earth began and Islam was formed, there has been the Sulṭānate. Allāh appointed the Sulṭān over you with all His Majesty and He dressed this majesty on you from the majesty of the heavenly Sulṭānate, but you throw this away and collect people from the markets, *bazaars*. Shame on you!

---

[62] Sūrat an-Nahl, 16:98-9.

Don’t Be Cursed by Angels!

Say, or may your tongue be tied, *“Bismillāhi ’r-Raḥmāni ’r-Raḥīm!”* Why do you speak without the *Bismillāh*? Are you ashamed to say, *“Bismillāhi ’r-Raḥmāni ’r-Raḥīm”*? So you are ashamed, aren't you? In that case, angels say, “May none of your work succeed, may you never find any goodness, may you never find any comfort, may you not be saved from troubles, sufferings and calamities!” All angels curse those who don’t say, *“Bismillāhi ’r-Raḥmāni ’r-Raḥīm.”* Even if you form a hundred parliaments and appoint all these hundreds of deputies and ministers, it still will not succeed.

O son, a cursed act cannot succeed! You collect some people to follow you and then say, “Here, our work succeeds.” Alright, go ahead and make it succeed if you can, make it succeed and we will see it!

Religion is the basis of the knowledge of Man. The *tadrisāt,* which they call ‘education’ now, is not based on religion and is zero. If you drive a stake into the straw, can you make a building on it? Shayṭān's teaching, which is the main trouble of the whole world today, says, “Don't construct the building here. Come and I will show you an easier place, come!” He brings them into a hayloft where he makes them drive a stake into the hay and says, “Here, this is a very strong building! It is new and this is the innovation you should follow. Leave the old castles, leave the old palaces. I will make you construct a building on top of the straw, as it is very easy. You can carry it anywhere you like and when you get hungry, you can also eat from that hay, and at that time you will become the man exactly in the shape I like!” which means, “You will become an animal for me.” Shayṭān says to the people, “Once you become animals for me, I will have plenty of hay. I will have so much that I can give you as much as you like.”

The Curse of Changing Currency from Gold and Silver to Paper

In the time of the sulṭān, there used to be gold and silver in the market. They removed it in WWI and called it the *“harb al-umūmi.”* Instead of gold they gave paper and said, “Spend this paper.” Spend with this paper? How will I spend with it? “Go and buy whatever you want from the market. We will put a seal on it and it will be valid everywhere.” Well, a paper will be worth the amount written on it, “1 Turkish *lira,* 5 Turkish *lira,* 10 Turkish *lira,* 20 Turkish *lira,* 50 Turkish *lira,* 100 Turkish *lira.”* Finally they wrote “200 Turkish *lira”* and felt ashamed. They say, “There is no higher number yet, but we want to print 1,000 Turkish *lira* banknotes also." So to make it four digits now, to write 1,000 and print such a banknote can make the people totally corrupt and crazy; it will put them into such a situation.

Therefore, now, in these peoples' *iqtisād*, which they call 'economy' now, all the nations went bankrupt because they are playing with paper money. What value does the paper money have? We may not go there now. So it means that they are not giving us what is valuable, because it is the teaching of Shayṭān. In the time of the Sulṭānate, everyone had gold and silver in their pockets. After this, there were reforms in the world and in the United States, as well. We said, "We should follow the world also. Why should we keep gold and silver? They are printing paper. They have the dollar, pound sterling, *draḥma* or *lira*. We may also create a Turkish *lira*. It belongs to us and we may also make a dollar, as the whole world follows it, but our dollar will be stronger than all others."

Why do you put it in the vault, why don't you give it to the people? Why are you hiding the gold and silver, for whom are you keeping it? If it is for the people let them have it and if not, why do you hide it? Why do you cheat the people? You show paper and say, "Its equivalent is in the vault." You lie! There is nothing in the vault. But they say like this, "It's equivalent is in the Central Bank, it is in this bank, in that bank, it is stored there." Why should you store it? Take it out and give the gold and silver to the people and release them to the streets! You can't even find a man who will sell his gold, he will keep it! But for paper money, he doesn't care and spends it recklessly.

So this is their "reform," the traps of the devil, the *shayṭāni* and evil traps. Why did you refuse Allāh's teaching for you? "Well, that one is religious, this one is national." It is a lie! One is heavenly, the other is *shayṭāni*! There are two sects now in the world: one is the heavenly system and the other is *shayṭāni*. Shayṭān makes foam and foam and foam, but it has no result! Foaming and foaming, it spilled over like the boiling milk and finished, only its watery part is left. Even that water is not left in those people now.

This is the trap set for the whole world now, "You will hide the gold and silver and give paper into the hands of people." No, you don't have the right for this! A person's service cannot be paid with paper. This is the wrong way. This is the way Shayṭān teaches people and deceives them.

Therefore, they don't find goodness—the Egyptians, Turks, Arabs and Americans—none of them, finished! This is the trap of the Shayṭān. The heavenly value is gold and silver. They hide it. No, you cannot hide it, as gold and silver is the right of the people. It should be in their hands, not in your vaults. Gold and silver should be in the pockets of the people. Don't say, "They are in the vault of the bank." Don't lie! This world went bankrupt because of lying. The people of this time fell into every trouble because of lies.

Therefore, O man of reason! O man who can think! They asked a philosopher, "Describe man." That philosopher said, "Man is a creature who can think." In other words, the animal who can think. Leave aside the animals, in our time there is no man left who thinks. Straighten yourselves, O people! Come to the right way. Don't fear to say *Haqq*! Don't fear, what can they do? They can only do what Allāh wants. As long as Allāh watches a person no one can touch even his hair!

Some people say, "How is this man? His back is strong. How?"

"This president backs him up," or, "That millionaire backs him up."

Leave the people! Say, "Allāh ﷻ backs up this man," meaning, *Allāh Dhul-Jalāl* is his guarantor. Fear such a person, fear him! If he touches you, not even ninety-nine doctors can find a cure for you. Don't think that to touch a Man of Allāh is an easy thing! Not even ninety-nine doctors can find a cure for you. These people should know Allāh! They should expel Shayṭān so that they become decent. They will find comfort in their *dunyā* as well as their *Akhirah* and they will be prosperous!

Let us say then, "*Bismillāhi 'r-Raḥmāni 'r-Raḥīm.*" O our Lord, may You accept us to Your servanthood! Although we have many defects and many sins, Your forgiveness is plenty O Lord! You made us, all these people, nations to Your Beloved ﷺ and these people, the people of this world are all running away from it! They will never find goodness. They will fight and crush each other. They will give each other's punishment with their own hands. This is not with money. Be a servant to Allāh and be saved in *dunyā*, in the grave and in *Akhirah*; if not, then you will suffer!

Amān, yā Rabbī! Tawbah, yā Rabbī! Tawbah, yā Rabbī! May You send us the ones who will teach us. We may say, "*Bismillāhi 'r-Raḥmāni 'r-Raḥīm.*" O our Lord, may You not expel us from Your servanthood. We are Your servants. May You forgive us, O Allāh! They didn't teach us. May those who didn't teach suffer the punishment wherever they are buried. Those who corrupted the people are all in the torment, in the Fire. May Allāh make us away from them and we should appreciate the fact that we are the nation of His Beloved ﷺ and say, "*Bismillāhi 'r-Raḥmāni 'r-Raḥīm. Lā ilāha illa-Llāh Sayyīdinā Muḥammadun Rasūlullāh* ﷺ*!*"

With the grant of Allāh Almighty, I will destroy the powers of unbelief in this world *inshā'Allāh*! I am of no use, cannot even go from here to there, but *inshā'Allāh* I will destroy! This is my intention. My goal is to destroy this Shayṭān and the order of Shayṭān. I want to live for this, I want to save human beings who are ridiculed by Shayṭān from his hands and even if it is little, I want to do what I can! Once the Lord helps, a person can correct even nine worlds!

Allāh! Tawbah, yā Rabbī. O Man, say, "*Bismillāhi 'r-Raḥmāni 'r-Raḥīm*" and walk right, then you will be saved!

Fātiḥah.

The First Salām is for Our Prophet ﷺ!

We may start with, *"Bismillāhi 'r-Raḥmāni 'r-Raḥīm." Anta Rabbu 'l-Jalīl,* our Lord, our beautiful Lord! What You granted Your Beloved, a drop from the oceans of *Jamāl* (Beauty) and *Kamāl* (Perfection) can make the Creation upside-down! *Mashā-Allāh, lā quwatta illā billāhi 'l-ʿAliyyu 'l-ʿAzhīm.* Grant us power, O Lord! Grant the power to Your Beloved and may we take from his oceans! A drop from the oceans of the Beloved whom You love and whom You called, "The servant I love," can make the Creation upside-down! Our Glorious Prophet, the Master of the Creation ﷺ!

O Believers! Listen, and we may also listen; we will listen and obey as whoever obeys will find safety, whoever obeys and accepts *al-Haqq* wears the dress of *nūr* and is dressed with the dress of wellness. When one is dressed with the dress of servanthood, we will be with those who are near to Allāh Almighty and who are worthy of being in His Divine Presence.

For what do we live? The value of those who live for *dunyā* is the same as the value of *dunyā,* and what is the value of *dunyā*? The Master of the Creation ﷺ gave an illustration of the world, as he said, *ad-dunyā jīfah,* "*Dunyā* is a carcass."[63] Whoever embraces the world finds trouble and punishment; he doesn't do any good in *dunyā,* nor does he receive any rank in *Akhirah.* A person who doesn't know what he is asked to do is not from Mankind!

As-salāmu ʿalaykum, O Believers! They are inspiring these few words to us. Whoever understands gets as much benefit as he understands and what can you do for one who doesn't understand? Whoever understands is a human being and whoever doesn't understand is an animal.

As-salāmu ʿalaykum! Look at how beautiful this is. What is the wish of the Believers for each other? It is said, "When two Believers see each other, they should greet with *salām.*" Greet each other with *salām,* but for whom should the first *salām* be? The first *salām* should be for our Prophet ﷺ, who is the Master of Creation. The first *salām* is for him!

---

[63] As cited on page 43.

As-salāmu ʿalayka yā ayyuha 'n-Nabī! At-tahiyyātu lillāhi wa 's-ṣalawātu wa 't-tayyibāt. As-salāmu ʿalayka wa ʿalā ālika wa ṣaḥābatika. Yā khayru khalqillāhi ayyuha 'n-Nabī!

Allāh Almighty is giving *salām* to our Prophet ﷺ. Look at the value and level of our Prophet. *As-salāmu ʿalayka ayyuha 'n-Nabī! At-tahiyyātu lillāhi wa 's-ṣalawātu wa 't-tayyibāt!* "*At-Tahīyyāt*" is the holy word which is in all the *salāms*; it is the most valuable and most worthy to Allāh among the words that servants say. "*At-tahiyyātu lillāh,*" and after that, "*at-tahiyyātu lillāhi wa 's-ṣalawātu wa 't-tayyibāt.*"

Secondly, Allāh Almighty gives *salām* to His Beloved, "*As-salāmu ʿalayka ayyuha 'n-Nabīyyu!*" *At-tahiyyātu lillāhi wa 's-ṣalawātu wa 't-tayyibāt. As-salāmu ʿalayka ayyuha 'n-Nabīyyu wa raḥmatullāhi wa barakātuh!*

Mashā'Allāh, the *salām* of Allāh Almighty to our Prophet ﷺ! Look at the rank of our Prophet ﷺ, which cannot be measured! *At-tahiyyatu lillāhi wa 's-ṣalawātu wa 't-tayyibāt, as-salāmu ʿalayka ayyuha 'n-Nabī.* O Glorious *Nabī* ﷺ! All *salāms*, all kinds of ranks belong to you, *wa 't-tayyibāt. At-tahiyyātu lillāhi wa 's-ṣalawātu wa 't-tayyibāt. As-salāmu ʿalayka ayyuha 'n-Nabī!*

After we presented the glorification of the Prophet ﷺ, "*At-tahiyyatu lillāhi wa 's-ṣalawātu wa 't-tayyibāt,*" Allāh Almighty gives *salām* to His Beloved, "*As-salāmu ʿalayka ayyuha 'n-Nabī! As-salāmu ʿalayka ayyuha 'n-Nabī!* O Glorious *Nabī*! May the *salām* be upon you." *Allāhu Akbar*! *As-salāmu ʿalayka ayyuha 'n-Nabīyyu wa raḥmatullāhi wa barakātuh. As-salāmu ʿalaynā wa ʿalā ʿibādī Llāhi 's-sālihīn. As-salāmu ʿalayka wa ʿalā ālika wa ṣaḥābatika.* May the *salām* be upon those who are near to you, upon your Companions ؓ and Nations! O Glorious Prophet, *salāms* to you!

When Allāh Dresses You

Allāh Almighty glorifies. Do you glorify our Prophet ﷺ, who is the origin of Creation? Do you ever think about him? Do you recite even one *ṣalawāt*? You don't. If you don't, then you have no value, you have no value! What is it that opens all these doors? What dresses all these virtues, beauties and perfection on Mankind? What dresses this dress on us is *Bismillāhi 'r-Raḥmāni 'r-Raḥīm.* Say, "*Bismillāhi 'r-Raḥmāni 'r-Raḥīm,*" and the most beautiful dress is dressed on you in the Presence of Allāh Almighty! Another person won't have the beauty of your dress, as there is no duplication in Allāh Almighty's Presence. *Al-Mubdīʿ! Al-Muʿīd*, "The Restorer of Life"! *Al-Mubdīʿu*, "The Originator" makes, but does not make carbon copies; everything is brand new, everything is beautiful and everything is in its perfection.

At-tahiyyātu lillāhi wa 's-ṣalawātu wa 't-tayyibāt, as-salāmu ʿalayka! Allāh Almighty grants so many other things along with *salām*. He grants so much to His Beloved. He ﷻ is Allāh *Jalla Jalālahu*, full with treasures! He ﷻ does not need them; they are for those who glorify our Prophet ﷺ, who is the Master of Creation, Muḥammad al-Mustafa ﷺ! Every day a new treasure opens to those who glorify him and show high respect for him, endless treasures!

What is the key of every treasure? It is *Bismillāhi 'r-Raḥmāni 'r-Raḥīm.* Whatever is in *dunyā* has no value just as *dunyā* has no value. Allāh Almighty opens a treasure for His servant when he says, "*Bismillāhi 'r-Raḥmāni 'r-Raḥīm.*" There is no one who can know the limits of the treasure Allāh opens. What He ﷻ gives to you is different, what He ﷻ gives to me is different, what He ﷻ gives to another one is different. The key of the treasure, O foolish people, why don't you ask what is the key of the treasures? It is *Bismillāhi 'r-Raḥmāni 'r-Raḥīm*! Say it and it opens for you! *Dunyā* is zero; it is for three days and on the fourth day they take you and bury you in your grave. You forgot this, you forgot about the day that they will bring and bury you in your grave, you don't think about it.

The Graves of Those Who Say "Bismillāhi 'r-Rahmāni 'r-Rahīm"

The Prophet ﷺ said:

كفى بالموت واعظاً يا عمر

If you want advice, death is enough, O ʿUmar![64]

Look at death and take advice, as no matter how much you strive for in *dunyā*, you will leave all of it there. They will put you inside the coffin that you didn't like in *dunyā*, that made you quiver when you saw it, and they

[64] The inscription on ʿUmar ibn al-Khattab's ring was, "Sufficient is death as an admonisher, O ʿUmar." (Ibn Kathir, *Al-Bidayah wal Nihayah*, 7/151)

will bring you to lay you in the earth. Don't forget that everybody will be buried in a grave! But the graves of those who say, *"Bismillāhi 'r-Raḥmāni 'r-Raḥīm"* are rose gardens, of which such a beauty has never been seen in *dunyā*. The grave of who says, *"Bismillāhi 'r-Raḥmāni 'r-Raḥīm,"* becomes from the Gardens of Paradise.

Why do you forget it, O foolish man? What will you find in *dunyā*? "We may drive a Rolls Royce." That is nothing! Having a luxurious brand of car and showing off with it, saying, "I have such a car," has no value. All the treasures of *dunyā* have no value. The day you enter your grave, how is your grave? The grave of who says, *"Bismillāhi 'r-Raḥmāni 'r-Raḥīm"* is a bed of roses. It opens and such a beauty is seen that it is impossible to imagine or be comprehended by the human mind. If Man tries to do it, he can't.

O ignorant people! Shame on you that you have forgotten your Lord, going after this trashy *dunyā* and killing each other. Who kills is a murderer and the torment of murderers starts in the grave. When they are put in the grave, whichever way he killed the other he shall be tormented the same way until the Day of Judgement! May Allāh protect us from the torment of the grave. Say, *"Bismillāhi 'r-Raḥmāni 'r-Raḥīm"* and your grave will be a garden from the Gardens of Paradise.

Dunyā is trash. A man who says the *Bismillāh* never becomes needy to anyone in *dunyā*. Allāh has never left a person who says, *"Bismillāhi 'r-Raḥmāni 'r-Raḥīm"* needy and Allāh Almighty has never tormented the ones who recite *ṣalawāt* on our Prophet ﷺ! It is for the honor of our Prophet that He ﷻ sent down the *Bismillāh* to him. Never stop saying it and your *dunyā* will become prosperous, also. You won't always be fifteen years old, twenty years old, twenty-five years old; day by day, your car is getting old, which you may change, but are you able to change your physical body?

The first place you will be hosted in your *Akhirah* journey is the grave. Did you prepare anything? Did you say, *"Bismillāhi 'r-Raḥmāni 'r-Raḥīm"*? If you said it, then a garden from the Gardens of Paradise is waiting for you there and the value of all the world is zero compared to it. The beauties of all the world are zero!

This dead one, I hear it, but you don't hear. If I don't hear, the other holy one hears it, that the dead one says, *"Bismillāhi 'r-Raḥmāni 'r-Raḥīm."* The moment he says the *Bismillāh,* his grave immediately opens and becomes a garden from the Gardens of Paradise. This is the *barakah* of

Bismillāhi 'r-Raḥmāni 'r-Raḥīm. He doesn't keep laying in it in the same way, it changes!

The Language of Accepted Worship is Arabic

O Believers! Don't forget this. Now people's concern is, "Can this be recited in Kurdish? Can it be recited in Turkish?" The language of worship is the language of the Holy Qur'ān. There is a fight now: this one says, "I will recite in Turkish," the other one says, "No, I will recite in Kurdish." The language of worship is Arabic!

إِنَّا أَنزَلْنَاهُ قُرْآنًا عَرَبِيًّا

Indeed, We have sent it down as an Arabic Qur'ān.[65]

Allāh is saying, "If you will address Us, you should address Us in the language of the Qur'ān." *Bismillāhi 'r-Raḥmāni 'r-Raḥīm* came in the Arabic language; it has honor, so you should worship with it. Merely saying, "I start in the Name of Allāh..." is imitated, it has no value. Does a person prefer the gold or a gold printed on paper? All these people think about is what is on the paper. You may change it, but it will not have the value of gold. "We recite the *khutbah* and we pray in Turkish." Okay, you may, but it is imitated and it won't be accepted as the language of worship is Arabic. Finished! You should recite in Arabic as much as you know.

How beautiful! Why don't you say, "*Bismillāhi 'r-Raḥmāni 'r-Raḥīm.*" Is there anyone who is not able to say, "*Bismillāhi 'r-Raḥmāni 'r-Raḥīm.*" Is there? Everybody can say it, they say "*Bismillāh.*" Now some top-rank government officials who are the sensible ones, when they open an institution and cut the ribbon with scissors they say, "May it be *mubarak. Bismillāhi 'r-Raḥmāni 'r-Raḥīm.*" Others want to make the *Bismillāh* forgotten, but the believer doesn't forget it; it cannot be made forgotten and they couldn't make it forgotten for one-hundred years! People still say, "*Bismillāh*" and confirm their servanthood to Allāh Almighty.

Then let us say, "*Bismillāhi 'r-Raḥmāni 'r-Raḥīm.*" O our Lord! Accept it from us. May they be unable to make us forget the *Bismillāh*, may they be unable to make us forget! May those who want us to forget disappear! We

---

[65] Sūrat Yusuf, 12:2.

are the servants of Allāh ﷻ and we accepted the Prophet ﷺ whom Allāh sent for us, and we accepted the Holy Qur'ān He ﷻ sent; therefore, we are Muslims. If you say, "I am Turkish," "Bosnian," "Arab," or "Albanian," it has no value. Are you Muslim? Say this and Muslims will be saved. Whoever says, "I am this, I am that" will be fertilizer, will be zero!

The Uniform of Believers is Bismillāh

O Believers! Today we may also say, *"Bismillāhi 'r-Raḥmāni 'r-Raḥīm."* We can be enlightened with the *nūr* of *Bismillāh* and we can be magnificent with the magnificence of *Bismillāh*. A uniform cannot give you honor. The uniform of a believer is *Bismillāhi 'r-Raḥmāni 'r-Raḥīm*. Say it and it will dress you with the dress of majesty! "This fashion, that fashion" is no good for you. Instead, say, *"Bismillāhi 'r-Raḥmāni 'r-Raḥīm"* and do not fear; you will be beautiful in *dunyā*, in the grave and in *mahshar*. *Yā Rabbī*! Save us from those who want to make us ugly. May they disappear!

O our Lord! May the honorable dress of *Bismillāh* that You dressed on us be permanent. Your Beloved ﷺ dressed the dress of *Bismillāh* on us, and the ones on the way of Your Beloved ﷺ are also dressing it on us. Say, *"Bismillāhi 'r-Raḥmāni 'r-Raḥīm"* and don't fear. Walk! But don't walk crooked or else you will get slapped. Who says the *Bismillāh* cannot do crooked things. Why does he not say the *Bismillāh*? Because he will do evil, so he is afraid to say the *Bismillāh*. If you are afraid, then don't do that bad thing. Start with the *Bismillāh*, and what you start with the *Bismillāh* may succeed, your day will become good in every aspect and your *Akhirah* will also be good. May Allāh dress you in the dress of majesty and dress us with the dress of faith. O our Lord! *Tubnā wa raja'nā ilayk. Tawbah, yā Rabbī!*

Then let us say, *"Bismillāhi 'r-Raḥmāni 'r-Raḥīm."* O our Lord! May You not deprive us of this mercy. May the mouths of those who don't teach us be closed and never open. O our Lord! You are the *Qādiru 'l-Muqtadir*, you can discipline them even with an ant. *Allāhu Akbar! Allāhu Akbar! Allāhu Akbar kabīrā wa 'l-ḥamdulillāhi kathīrā wa subḥānallāhi bukratan wa asīlā. Thumma salātu wa 's-salāmu 'alayka ayyuha 'n-Nabīyyu wa raḥmatullāhi wa barakātuh.* We are in need of your compassion and intercession!

حول حالنا الى احسن الحال يا محول الحول والأحوال

O Transformer of States! Turn our situation to the best of situations![66]

Don't run in the streets, don't be like animals, be like Man, be dignified. Don't be animals, but be Man so you will be in goodness. O our Lord, You know! We have surrendered to You and may we be sacrificed in Your Beloved's ﷺ way only, may we not forget the *Bismillāh,* may we be sacrificed in the way of Allāh and in the way of the Prophet ﷺ who taught us the *Bismillāh*

Recite this *Bismillāh* and be saved; if not, all of them will vanish. *SubḥānAllāh wa 'l-ḥamdulillāh wa lā ilāha illa-Llāh. Allāhu Akbar, Allāhu Akbar, wa lillāhi 'l-ḥamd!*

Reciting "Bismillāhi 'r-Rahmāni 'r-Rahīm" Removes Troubles

Bismillāhi 'r-Raḥmāni 'r-Raḥīm. Say the *Bismillāh* at least seven times, or forty times, or seventy times or one-hundred times. Say the *Bismillāh* and see how your situation will be. How will your situation be? Will you have any troubles left? Will you have any hardships left on you? No!

O People! Don't forget your humanity! Shayṭān wants to make you forget your humanity, and what happens when you forget? What happens when Man forgets his humanity? He becomes Shayṭān, and what is the goal of Shayṭān all about? To make Man *shayṭān* like himself. This is what his goal is all about, to make people *shayṭāns.* He doesn't want Man to make servanthood for Allāh. "You are not Allāh's servant," he says, "Be with me." So they will be *shayṭān* like him also and do all kinds of dirty things. Shame on them! Shame on them! A person who says the *Bismillāh* can't do evil, he can't think evil and he can't oppress anyone. Anyone who is beyond this will be left in fire in their graves. *Amān, yā Rabbī*! The keys to the knowledge which will teach us such things are in *Bismillāhi 'r-Raḥmāni 'r-Raḥīm.* Listen to who says the *Bismillāh* and leave who doesn't, as they are the tribe of Shayṭān, may they vanish.

Let us say, "*Bismillāhi 'r-Raḥmāni 'r-Raḥīm.*" Today is like this also. Religion is advice; there is no politics in religion. Religion has no political connections, no! There is no politics in religion, religion is religion, it is the

66 A *du'ā*; supplication.

order of Allāh ﷻ! You should keep it and your work succeeds. If you don't say it, you will not find any goodness in *dunyā* or in *Akhirah. Amān, yā Rabbī! Tawbah, yā Rabbī! Tawbah, astaghfirullāh.*

Let us say, "*Bismillāhi 'r-Raḥmāni 'r-Raḥīm.*" Today may also open with the *Bismillāh.* May you find goodness; who listen finds goodness, so may they have goodness. Who does not listen may suffer what will come on them. *Amān, yā Rabbī! Tawbah, yā Rabbī.* For the honor of Your Beloved, forgive us and send us Your servants who will show us, teach us the right ways.

May Allāh show us good days also, may we be granted to meet Mahdi ﷺ. We want power and it will come *inshā'Allāh.* There is no chance for the oppressors as starting from today, I have locked them! I am nothing, but I locked them. They make me say like this. I will imprison the oppressors! They will see if it will happen or not. *Tawbah, yā Rabbī! Tawbah astaghfirullāh!* Be upon safety. Send *salāms.*

Fātiḥah.

The Riches of Qarun

As-salāmu ʿalaykum, O servants of Allāh. *Marhaban bikum, marhaba,* greetings to you! *Madad, madad.* There are holy ones who are the *Ahl al-Imdād,* who can give support, and whatever is granted from the holy ones to us is, according to our situation, only a spot. So we sit here and speak of them as they are making us speak.

We may say and open the door, the key to every door is *Bismillāhi 'r-Raḥmāni 'r-Raḥīm.* Say it, how beautiful it is! When one says, "*Bismillāhi 'r-Raḥmāni 'r-Raḥīm,*" there are no troubles, no *qaswat,* hardness left for that person. There is no hopelessness, no burdens, no ugliness or sufferings left for him. Allāh! Let us say, "*Bismillāhi 'r-Raḥmāni 'r-Raḥīm, Bismillāhi 'r-Raḥmāni 'r-Raḥīm, Bismillāhi 'r-Raḥmāni 'r-Raḥīm!*"

Whoever remembers the Holy Name of Allāh Almighty and does not find comfort, it means that person has a big trouble. Some say that *dunyā* is the land of difficulties and is not something to be sought. No! They call it "the land of difficulties." Every step you take in, *dunyā* makes you to stumble over something, it gives you a trouble. Why? A person who runs after *dunyā* will be humiliated, even if he has as much wealth as Qarūn. Qarūn is a symbol of wealth for Mankind, that a big group of animals will carry the keys of his treasuries and the largest of the keys was as thick as a man's finger. So much treasure! What happened? What did these treasures do for him? They humiliated him! He was humiliated. The wealth he had was not given to anyone else and what did this wealth do to him? The Earth swallowed him, he was humiliated! He sank into the Earth along with his treasures, because he didn't enter the service of the Almighty, *Al-Bari* ﷻ.

He came to the great Prophet Musa ﵇ in pride and said, "I have all these treasures, so I don't need to listen to you or to keep your orders. I live as I like! My treasures are countless." He kept saying, "Me, me, me. I have this, I have that!" Even if the whole world belonged to him, what good would it do? If the whole world turned into precious stones and belonged to him, what was going to happen? Here, who is the richest man in the world? Qarūn. When someone is very wealthy, people say, "He is rich like Qarūn." Did we say the *Bismillāh,* "*Bismillāhi 'r-Raḥmāni 'r-Raḥīm?*" Say this and have no fear and your doings will be solid.

Look, it is the word of our Prophet ﷺ:

كل أمر ذي بال لا يبدأ فيه ببسم الله الرحمن الرحيم فهو أقطع أو (فهو ابتر)

Any action which does not begin with 'Bismillāhi 'r-Raḥmāni 'r-Raḥīm' is cut off; it has no continuity.[67]

It doesn't produce, it doesn't bring any generation, nothing comes after him, nothing! *Abtar* means "barren," it won't have anything, no child or generations. Allāh Almighty is warning His servants that 124,000 prophets came, all of them to make people say *"Allāh."* Shame on those who refused to say *"Allāh!"* They say, "Shayṭān shows us the beautiful way, he shows us the entertainment and fun part of the life of *dunyā*; he shows us how we will enjoy and take pleasure in *dunyā*." Then what happens? He throws you into a filth from which no doctors or judges can save you! There is no one who can answer your cries; they reach to the skies, but there is no one to answer because you didn't care for your Lord and say, *"Bismillāhi 'r-Raḥmāni 'r-Raḥīm"* and, "I am the servant of Allāh, I am created to make servanthood for Allāh."

What have you been created for? He answers, "I have been created for my pleasure, to collect more and more pleasure and wealth." Here is the example of Qarūn: he collected and it collapsed on his head. The Earth swallowed him with his treasures, but the people in this time are not thinking about such things, they are all in meaningless pursuit.

To Live a Simple Life is Better

America says, "I am rich." Russia says, "I am richer." Iran says, "No, I have treasures." The ones in *Hijāz* say, "No, we have petrol under the ground." Before, in our times it was known as "lamp oil." In the old times, we had no electricity and we lit candles and lamps everywhere, in the street and neighborhoods. I remember there was an old Greek man who called, "Petroleum, here is lamp oil!" He carried a gallon in a tin container and he had a scale to measure it. The small, old man made his living by selling it, enough to manage the whole month.

---

[67] Aḥmad, al-Musnad.

Mashā'Allāh the ones now who are on the same way as that man who sold lamp oil are so proud, thinking, "We have this much petrol, we have this much lamp oil!" May it be poured over their heads! Now all of Arabia and Iran (is like this) and only poor Turks are left. They cannot sell lamp oil, but they buy it. They also make it run through the pipes and we buy from the free side. Iran is proud of all its kingdoms and emirates and so on. In what do they take pride? Calling, "Petroleum, I sell petrol!" Look, what I remember from my childhood is a lesson for the people. That man made his living out of it and at the same time, we had simple lamps and candles in our homes. Our life was simple, but sweet. At that time we needed perhaps five things, now we need five-hundred! Whatever you do, it needs electricity or petrol. May those who are called 'oil rich' fall into it, as they got rich from oil and what did they do?

Like Qarūn saved all his wealth and went deep under earth. Our people don't draw any lessons from the past, they don't teach the history, they are only occupying themselves with all kinds of things in this Shayṭān box (TV) from morning to night and from night until morning. It shows their lives, *lā hawla wa lā quwatta!*

Sayyīdinā Ibrahim ibn Adham, may Allāh make his abode Paradise, had twelve-thousand dogs to watch his herds, *Hashakum*. He was very rich. Most of the old kings and sulṭāns had an interest in hunting as it is *halāl*, permitted. One day he went hunting with his entourage, as it was a custom for the sulṭāns and he, too, is a sulṭān. He was hunting like the wind with his entourage in the deserts and in the forests, but his time had come.

When he was riding full force at top speed, from one side a voice came to his ears, "O Sulṭān, are you created for this?" The words on this side finished. Then a voice came to his second ear, *Aw bi hadha 'l-umirt? Āli hadha khuliqt, aw bi hadha 'l-umirt?* "Are you created or ordered for this?" It is said that he stopped his horse and returned to the palace, as this was enough for him. Ibrahim ibn Adham ق, Sulṭān Ibrahim, has a majestic mosque in Latakia. *Alḥamdulillāh*, I visited Sulṭān Ibrahim ﺽ, the Holy One. He left everything, saying, "I don't need them, this word is enough for me."

Indeed, people do not know why they are created; they do not search as they do not want to learn that this is for all people. O People! Are you created for these fights and wars?

Allāh Almighty has said:

وَمَا خَلَقْتُ الْجِنَّ وَالْإِنسَ إِلَّا لِيَعْبُدُونِ مَا أُرِيدُ مِنْهُم مِّن رِّزْقٍ وَمَا أُرِيدُ أَن يُطْعِمُونِ

I have only created jinn and human beings so that they may worship Me. No sustenance do I require of them, nor do I require that they should feed Me.[68]

Where are you, O People? You are killing, burning and destroying each other and yet, you claim to be human. The animals in the jungles are better than you! They don't take pride in their wealth or power, they just wander in the jungle. This is the civilization of today's people, this is what they follow. Where did it take you in the end? This is the way of Shayṭān and Shayṭān brought them to this in the end and made them fall into this deadlock. Now there is such a blind knot that it cannot be untied. How can you untie it? Where can you untie it? *Lā hawla wa lā quwatta! Lā hawla wa lā quwatta!*

May Allāh grant us His servanthood! May we be servants to our Lord. The honored life is this servanthood for Allāh. O People! Stand for the worship of Allāh! Allāh grants you the sweetest life. Your *dunyā* and *Akhirah* will be prosperous. *Yā Rabbī! Tubnā wa raja'na ilayk. Tawbah yā Rabbī, tawbah astaghfirullāh*!

Our Egyptians don't understand, our Westerners don't understand, the ones in *Hijāz* and in *Shām* don't understand. There is no one who understands in Turkey, Iran, India or China. Shayṭān made people to fall into a fight, asking, "With which weapon will we finish each other? With the chemical weapons! We can't handle them, so we will poison the air from above and all of them will be poisoned!" Is it you who granted them life? Who gave you the authority to kill these people? You shameless ones, you who don't fear from Allāh! I will discipline you with such a discipline that whoever sees it and hears it will know and remember it! I will show them the result of being animals of Shayṭān!

---

[68] Sūrat adh-Dhariyat, 51:56-57.

All the world has turned into a slaughterhouse and has fallen into total madness, when they all cut, break, crush and kill each other! They have gone completely crazy. Someone asked how many kinds of craziness are there? There are three kinds. What are they? They are crazy, totally crazy and totally and utterly crazy! Previously there were crazy ones and very few totally crazy ones, but people now passed over these stages to the third one and have become utterly crazy. They say, "We are kings, we are presidents!" Say this when you go to your graves!

O our Lord! May You grant us repentance. May You send us a sulṭān who will be our master, for the honor of Your Beloved. What can we do? Our word doesn't reach from here to the door! *O Allāh, O Allāh, tawbah yā Rabbī, tawbah yā Rabbī, tawbah yā Rabbī!*

Whichever home you go to, everyone has all kinds of troubles because they are without the *Bismillāh*. Some of them have a remedy and some of them do not. The least of their troubles is, their son and daughter went to college but they can't find a job. This is it. There is no one who says, "We are studying for Allāh, let us be in the service of Allāh." They try to be employed by the government and get paid without doing much.

May Allāh grant us a share from this advice and may we know ourselves. *Tawbah yā Rabbī, tawbah yā Rabbī, tawbah astaghfirullāh! Shukr, yā Rabbī.*

Amān, yā Rabbī. This is a strange *ṣuḥbah*. May Allāh give you safety. May our day be good. May we live in the Way of Allāh. May we leave *dunyā* in the Way of Allāh, *yā Rabbī*. May our only worry be Your servanthood, O Lord! May we not be crushed in troubles! Let us be busy with Your servanthood. How beautiful! O Lord, forgive us for the honor of Your Beloved. We ask for your intercession, O *Rasūlullāh* ﷺ!

Fātiḥah.

The Key to Paradise

As-salāmu 'alaykum. We woke up with goodness and may we reach the evening with goodness, *inshā'Allāh.* Ask goodness from Allāh Almighty. We should know what we want so our day may be good and our work, also. We have reached a new day, so our life has decreased and we have come closer to the *Akhirah* by one more day.

As-salāmu 'alaykum, O Believers! *Salām* be on the great Prophet ﷺ, *as-salātu wa 's-salām* be upon him. He is our master, he is the Master of Creation, he is the Prophet who brought down the Divine Lights from the *Malakūt. Mashā'Allāh. Allāhumma salli 'alā Sayyīdinā Muḥammad wa 'alā ālihi wa ṣaḥbihi wa sallam.*

What can we do? We may say a few words so that relief comes on us today, strength comes, an opening comes, and joy comes to us. Okay then, for this let us open the door of our *ṣuḥbah.* With what do we open the door? *"Bismillāhi 'r-Raḥmāni 'r-Raḥīm." Yā Rabbī, shukr. Yā Rabbī, shukr.* O Lord! *Yā Rabbī, shukr.* O Lord! *Shukr.* Our Lord Who teaches us and informs us about the *Bismillāh,* and Who dresses us with the Divine Light of that *Bismillāh.* O our Lord!

ربي يسر ولا تعسر ,ربي تمم بالخير

O my Lord, make things easier for me, do not make things difficult for me.[69]

Bismillāhi 'r-Raḥmāni 'r-Raḥīm. We should begin all our work with the *Bismillāh* so that it will be easy, it will have *barakah,* and the doors of goodness will open. Without saying the *Bismillāh* the doors of goodness do not open, not a single door opens in *dunyā,* nor in *Akhirah.* The doors of Paradise open with the *Bismillāh* and people enter, and without the *Bismillāh* one cannot enter Paradise! *Mashā'Allāh.* When a person says the *Bismillāh,* his day goes well; it will be a happy day, a blessed day, goodness opens for him, Divine Light comes on his face, health comes to his body, *barakah* comes on his work and *khayr* and *hasanat* come on his children.

---

[69] A *du'ā*; supplication.

O our Allāh! You granted us to remember Your Holy Name, *Bismillāhi 'r-Raḥmāni 'r-Raḥīm*. What a great and magnificent holy verse this is:

إِنَّهُ مِن سُلَيْمَانَ وَإِنَّهُ بِسْمِ اللَّهِ الرَّحْمَنِ الرَّحِيمِ

Verily it is from Sulaymān and verily it begins with the Name of Allāh, The Beneficent, The Merciful.[70]

The *Bismillāh* is mentioned in the Holy Qur'ān. In the beginning of Prophet Sulayman's order to the palace of Bilqis, the Queen of Sheba, is written, *Innahu min Sulaymān wa innahu Bismillāhi 'r-Raḥmāni 'r-Raḥīm.* It is from Sulayman but, *wa innahu Bismillāhi 'r-Raḥmāni 'r-Raḥīm.* The great Prophet Sulayman ﷺ started with "*Bismillāhi 'r-Raḥmāni 'r-Raḥīm,*" as did all the prophets! Prophet Muḥammad ﷺ started with the *Bismillāh.* The most valuable thing that opens all doors and completes all our good acts in *dunyā* is "*Bismillāhi 'r-Raḥmāni 'r-Raḥīm.*" The eight doors of Heavens open with *Bismillāhi 'r-Raḥmāni 'r-Raḥīm.* For this, we should also say, "*Bismillāhi 'r-Raḥmāni 'r-Raḥīm.*" Allāh ﷻ granted this to His servants in *dunyā,* to the Believers, so that all their doings will succeed.

This is the greatest treasure, *Bismillāhi 'r-Raḥmāni 'r-Raḥīm.* What a great honor is this! The honor of whoever forgets this is at zero level and none of their doings succeed. Can a plane fly if you don't put gas in it? It will stop and not take off. What is it that Man is in need of? He is in need of spiritual power. If we don't have spiritual power, we will be like the plane waiting in the airport with no gas in it. How can it take off? So it has everything, but there is one thing missing.

Protesting in the Streets Will Never Save You

People are like this, too: we have everything, but there is one thing missing. This is because we don't say the *Bismillāh.* When you say the *Bismillāh,* Creation is fueled and becomes full so it takes off and flies. There is no one who says the *Bismillāh* and cannot complete a good act; the *Bismillāh* completes every good act! Don't forget the *Bismillāh.*

---

[70] Sūrat an-Naml, 27:30.

نَسُوا اللهَ فَنَسِيَهُمْ

They have forgotten Allāh, so He has forgotten them.[71]

In the Holy Qur'ān. Allāh Almighty informs us about the terrible situation of His .From where did all these troubles and calamities come to the people? They are asking, "Why so many disasters are happening like this?" Because they forgot Allāh and so Allāh left them. He ﷻ) left them! Allāh does not forget, but He left them in this forgotten state; otherwise, His support reaches instantly.

He ﷻ is whipping constantly so that we remember our Lord, but there is no one who remembers Him. They run in the streets like wild animals, women and men, and their men shout and scream (in protest marches and anti-government strikes). What do you seek in the street? What is it that you are looking for? Don't you have mosques? Why do you go out and scream in the streets? All of you could go to your mosques and say, "O our Lord! *Najjinā mimā nakhāf.* Save us from what we fear, our Lord!" You should have entered your mosques and said, "O our Lord! Save us from the oppressors." Go to the mosque and say this. Who are you calling to in the street? You shout and scream and they fire at you. Why do they fire? So that we come to our senses and go to the mosque!

Yā Mufattiha 'l-abwāb, iftahlana khayra 'l-bāb. O our Lord! You are the One Who opens all the doors for us. Open the doors for us, O our Lord. We have no hope from those, not from the Arabs, nor from their princes or kings is there any benefit to us, and neither from America nor from Russia does any benefit come to us. Call, "O our Lord! *Najjinā mimā nakhāf.* Save us from what we fear. Save us, O Lord!"

Why don't you say this instead of running in the streets? Is such behavior in Islam? Is it suitable for the Muslims? Shame on such Muslims who leave the mosques and scream in the streets! No, this is the wrong way. It is the wrong way!

The right way is to go and find the Presence of Allāh in the mosques and call, "*Yā Rabbī*! *Yā Rabbanā*! *Najjinā mimā nakhāf.* Make us safe from what we fear, O our Lord!"

---

[71] Sūrat at-Tawbah, 9:67.

Why do you run in the streets? What kind of Muslims are you? Then they say, "You didn't help us." Not even the seven (most powerful) countries can help you! You should go to the mosques, you should stand in the Presence of Your Lord and you should beg, "*Yā Muhawwil al-hawli wa 'l-ahwāl, hawwil hālanā ila ahsani 'l-hāl*. O Lord, Who changes the states of Man from one to another! May You make us upon the best *hāl*. O Lord! May You send Your beautiful servants. O Lord! *Bismillāhi 'r-Raḥmāni 'r-Raḥīm*. O Lord! Open Your doors of Mercy. Send from Your lions. *Yā Ghāliban Ghayra Maghlūb*. We seek refuge in You, for You cannot be defeated, You are the Absolute Victorious! Send us support!"

Like this. Can He not send His support? When they got stuck in the Battle of Badr, the Glorious Prophet ﷺ prayed, "Send us support!" One thousand angels came down. Then? *Bi-khamsati ālāfin*, "five-thousand of them," *musawwimīn*, "Having marks of distinction," with turbans on their heads and its loose end hanging on the backs. He ﷻ says, "I send support with such angels." But no, there is no need for it now, now these angels will come down, but they didn't come down at that time, He ﷻ delayed it. "If My servants call in this time of corruption, I will send down five-thousand for the honor of My Beloved!"

يُمْدِدْكُمْ رَبُّكُم بِخَمْسَةِ آلافٍ مِّنَ الْمَلآئِكَةِ مُسَوِّمِينَ

Indeed, if you remain firm and act right, even if the enemy should rush here upon you in hot haste, your Lord would help you with five-thousand angels wearing turbans with tails.[72]

Only one angel can make everything upside-down, but He ﷻ said, "I will send five-thousand," in His Magnificence. Now these five-thousand will come with Mahdi ؑ. Allāh Almighty will show how He protects Islam, how He protects the *Haqq*, the True Religion. *Allāh Dhu 'l-Jalāl* will show these heedless Muslims, some of whom say "America" and some who say "Russia (will save us)!" Shame on them! Shame on their kings, princes and presidents, also. Shame on them that they forgot Allāh! They are the disliked group. They say, "China is like this (better than us), Russia is like this, America is like this." What is our business with them? Do you not have

[72] Sūrat Āli-'Imrān, 3:125.

your Allāh, that you say, "*Yā Rabbī,*" and raise your hands? Shame on you! There are forty *walis* of Allāh in *Shām*. If they called them once, they made *Shām* upside-down and would not let the tyrants approach, but because of our heedlessness and because we forgot the *Bismillāh*, the one who forgets the *Bismillāh* has forgotten Allāh!

Yā Allāh! You are the Sulṭān! Send us a sulṭān. May these rubbish people go away. They corrupted everything. They are not listening to the Holy Qur'ān, they are not reading it, they are running and screaming in the streets. Shame on them! Say, *Bismillāhi 'r-Raḥmāni 'r-Raḥīm. Bismillāhi 'r-Raḥmāni 'r-Raḥīm.*" *Sayfullāh al-Maslūl* (the Drawn Sword of Allāh) draws the sword if they say, "O our Lord!" and five-thousand angels come down. There is no fear from their cannons, rifles, missiles, or museums.

O Muslims! Come to Islam! If not, this world will grind you and throw you away!

وَالَّذِينَ آمَنُوا أَشَدُّ حُبًّا لِلَّهِ

But those of faith are overflowing in their love for Allāh.[73]

Allāh Protects All Who Follow His Advice

Allāh Almighty will bring a people whom He will love and they will love Him! Why don't you be from them, O Muslims! O people of Egypt, the people of Hijāz, the people of *Shām* and Turkistan, the people of Turkey, the Iranians! Why don't you know Allāh and call to Him? Why do you kill each other, for which reason? For a person to sit on a seat. He may not sit! It is not your power that will take him out of his position. If Allāh likes He can take him out instantly, but because you deserve it He inflicted him upon you. Therefore, repent!

يَا أَيُّهَا الَّذِينَ آمَنُوا تُوبُوا إِلَى اللَّهِ تَوْبَةً نَصُوحًا عَسَى رَبُّكُمْ أَن يُكَفِّرَ عَنكُمْ سَيِّئَاتِكُمْ وَيُدْخِلَكُمْ جَنَّاتٍ تَجْرِي مِن تَحْتِهَا الْأَنْهَارُ يَوْمَ لَا يُخْزِي اللَّهُ النَّبِيَّ وَالَّذِينَ آمَنُوا مَعَهُ نُورُهُمْ يَسْعَى بَيْنَ أَيْدِيهِمْ وَبِأَيْمَانِهِمْ يَقُولُونَ رَبَّنَا أَتْمِمْ لَنَا نُورَنَا وَاغْفِرْ لَنَا إِنَّكَ عَلَى كُلِّ شَيْءٍ قَدِيرٌ

O Believers! Turn to Allāh with sincere repentance in the hope that your Lord will remove from you your ills and admit you to Gardens beneath which Rivers flow (on) the Day that Allāh will not permit to be humiliated the Prophet and those who

---

[73] Sūrat al-Baqara, 2:165.

believe with him! Their Light will run forward before them and by their right hands, while they say, "Our Lord! Perfect our Light for us, and grant us forgiveness, for You have power over all things."[74]

Tubna wa raja'na 'alayk, yā Rabbī. Forgive us, O Lord!

الَّذِينَ يَسْتَمِعُونَ الْقَوْلَ فَيَتَّبِعُونَ أَحْسَنَهُ أُوْلَئِكَ الَّذِينَ هَدَاهُمُ اللَّهُ وَأُوْلَئِكَ هُمْ أُوْلُوا الْأَلْبَابِ

Those who listen (closely) to all that is said and follow the best of it, it is they whom God has graced with His guidance, and it is they who are (truly) endowed with insight! [75]

Allāh protects those who listen to His Words and to His advice and who listens to the advice of His Prophet ﷺ. He ﷻ is with them, but you who leave Him are with Shayṭān! You made (political) parties. Shame on you, O you who claim to be Muslims! It asks for a sulṭān. The first obligation on the Muslims after the Prophet ﷺ is, "You must have a *khalifah,*" one person who rules the whole Islamic world, not a thousand people. You sit there and say, "I rule," but when you abandon justice you will suffer in *dunyā* and in *Akhirah*!

O Lord! We are helpless servants. We are saying, *"Bismillāhi 'r-Raḥmāni 'r-Raḥīm."* O our Lord! May You accept our *Bismillāh*. These people should say the *Bismillāh* at least forty times daily and they will be saved. Some of them are after lamp oil, petrol, some of them are after natural gas, and some of them are after gold. Leave this. Look to the order of Allāh, *wa 'ahsinu,* "Do good."

إِنَّ اللَّهَ يُحِبُّ الْمُحْسِنِينَ

Truly Allāh loves the doers of good.[76]

Allāh loves the good doers. What are you waiting for, why do you save and store up? Don't store, give! Give for your life. Say, *"Bismillāhi 'r-Raḥmāni 'r-Raḥīm,"* and treasures will open. O Lord! May You forgive us. *Tawbah, yā Rabbī. Tawbah, yā Rabbī.* In this holy month of *Mawlid,* open! Give your

---

[74] Sūrat al-Qalam, 66:8.
[75] Sūrat az-Zumar, 39:18.
[76] Sūrat al-Baqara, 2:195.

treasures, give for Allāh. On *Yawm al-Mahshar*, the Day of Resurrection, they will say, "Bravo for you!" Otherwise the *zabāniyah* will seize you by the collar and will throw you into the Hellfire. May Allāh forgive us. *Fātiḥah.*

We should say, *"Bismillāhi 'r-Raḥmāni 'r-Raḥīm,"* and blow it onto ourselves. Say, *"Bismillāhi 'r-Raḥmāni 'r-Raḥīm. Bismillāhi 'Lladhī lā yadurru ma'a ismihi shay'un fi 'l-arḍi wa lā fi 's-sama'i wa Huwa 's-Samī'u 'l-'Alīm."* Muslims should put on their heads the crown of Islam (turban). Nothing will come on their heads. Ladies should not go out with their heads uncovered, dressing up and putting on makeup. They should cover their heads. Nothing will come on them from the Heavens. We don't pay attention and we don't accept advice either; there is no one to accept advice. They are shouting and screaming in the streets and doing crazy things. They will kill each other. Is it the order of Allāh for us to kill each other? Shame on them.

O our Lord! May You send us the master for the honor of Your Beloved. Send a sulṭān, O our Lord! Send the Mahdi ﷵ of whose coming Your Beloved gave the glad tidings. We have no strength left, O Lord! *Tawbah, yā Rabbī. Tawbah, yā Rabbī. Tawbah, astaghfirullāh.* May You lift this burden from us. For the honor of Your Beloved, send us support, O Lord. We wait for these five-thousand angels; they will come with Mahdi ﷵ. Send them, O Lord! *Tubna wa raja'na ilayk, yā Rabbana.* Let us say, *"Bismillāhi 'r-Raḥmāni 'r-Raḥīm,"* so that all doors of goodness open and all doors of calamity close. Say, *"Bismillāhi 'r-Raḥmāni 'r-Raḥīm!"*

O Muslims! Don't go out with your heads uncovered. Go out in Islamic dress and nothing will come on you. O Ladies! If you go out with your heads uncovered, dressing up and putting on makeup, you will suffer in *dunyā* as well as inside your graves and neither your king nor your *mulūk* can save you. *Tawbah, yā Rabbī. Tawbah, yā Rabbī. Tawbah, astaghfirullāh.* I repent and for your own situation also, I repent. *Tawbah, ya Rabbī. Tawbah, yā Rabbī.* Instead of being busy with Your servanthood we are trying to burn and destroy each other. Shame on people. This is not the honor of humanity, the honor of humanity is to make service to their Lord, it is not with fighting.

O Muslims! Pull yourselves together before something comes on you. *Tawbah, astaghfirullāh.* Let us say, *"Bismillāhi 'r-Raḥmāni 'r-Raḥīm. Lā ilāha illa-Llāh Sayyīdinā Muḥammadun Rasūlullāh."* We ask your intercession, O

Rasūlullāh ﷺ! *Fātiḥah.* O Lord! I only want to see *Shām* open and Sayyīdinā Mahdi ؑ come, this is it, I don't want anything else. I have no business with *dunyā* anymore!

As-salāmu ʿalaykum. Salām upon those who listen. Whoever doesn't listen will suffer what will come on his head. *Allāh, Allāh. Fātiḥah.*

"Remember Me and I Will Remember You"

We may say, "*Bismillāhi 'r-Raḥmāni 'r-Raḥīm.*" May Allāh ﷻ not make us without religion or understanding. Our tongues should say "Allāh" and *ṣalawāt* for the pure Prophet, Aḥmadi Muḥammad al-Mustafa ﷺ! Our tongues should always recite *ṣalawāt* for the Beloved of Allāh Almighty, the *ṣalawāt ash-sharīf,* and we may say as the Prophet ﷺ said:

كل أمر ذي بال لا يبدأ فيه ببسم الله الرحمن الرحيم فهو أقطع أو (فهو ابتر)

Any action which does not begin with 'Bismillāhi 'r-Raḥmāni 'r-Raḥīm' is cut off; it has no continuity.[77]

The saying of "*dhiy bālin*" is for teaching us; *dhiy bāl* is an important, matter or something of value. Allāh Almighty orders us, "Do beautiful acts, perform good deeds." The glory of the believer is in doing beautiful actions, doing beautiful service, doing beautiful deeds, and doing beautiful servanthood, because servanthood requires beautiful service and a servant is the one who makes good service. Who strives to do foolish, meaningless things is far away from servanthood. The things a servant does are solid and firm, he doesn't do a rotten thing. Why? Because he will say the *Bismillāh*, and then the service he does is clean, it is firm.

A believer's work cannot be corrupt, it will be clean. A believer has *nūr* on his face and joy in his heart. Also, a believer does not live a sad life, a believer is happy, a believer is the owner of good deeds and he is in the first class when making service for Allāh Almighty!

May Allāh ﷻ not remove us from His servanthood! *Bismillāhi 'r-Raḥmāni 'r-Raḥīm.* O our Lord! May You forgive us. Don't make us forget to remember Your Holy Name!

نَسُوا اللَّهَ فَنَسِيَهُمْ

They have forgotten Allāh, so He has forgotten them.[78]

---

[77] Aḥmad, al-Musnad.

[78] Sūrat at-Tawbah, 9:67.

Deeds Reflect Radiance and Darkness on Our Faces

They forgot Allāh and Allāh leaves them, forgotten! Who runs away from Allāh becomes forgotten, and a person whom Allāh forgets cannot find goodness, just as a nation that does not accept Allāh cannot find goodness Anyone who does not keep the order of Allāh before everything else cannot find goodness.

What does he become? He becomes the animal of Shayṭān. Shayṭān bridles and mounts that person, but when you say, "*Bismillāhi 'r-Raḥmāni 'r-Raḥīm*," Shayṭān can't put a bridle on you! Shayṭān wants to make human beings his animals to do all kinds of dirty things. Those who do dirty, dishonored things are the animals of Shayṭān. A person with a dark face is the animal of Shayṭān, and a person who has a clean face with *nūr* is the servant of his Lord and from the nation of our Prophet ﷺ.

You should be careful with this, it should be taught with which deed do people's faces shine and which deeds darken their faces? The faces of people today, ninety-nine percent of them are dark and who looks at their faces finds no goodness, and who works for them has no goodness! *Amān, yā Rabbī! Amān, yā Rabbī*! May our Lord save us from being animals to Shayṭān.

Allāh Almighty sent us His Most Beloved ﷺ so that we will always know our way, our path, and how to attain acceptance of our Lord Almighty. They are strong. Whenever a nation kept Allāh, then Allāh kept them. Whosoever does not keep Allāh, Allāh Almighty leaves them. *Nasū 'Llāha fa nasiyahum*, "Who forgets Allāh becomes forgotten." Say, "Allāh!" How should we say it? Say, "*Bismillāhi 'r-Raḥmāni 'r-Raḥīm*," when you get up, when you sit, when you work, when you do anything. Put "*Bismillāh*" signs inside your home, put "*Bismillāhi 'r-Raḥmāni 'r-Raḥīm*" signs everywhere and don't fear as neither stones will rain on you nor will you get stuck under snow or taken prisoner by the enemy!

Bismillāhi 'r-Raḥmāni 'r-Raḥīm. We should hang its signs everywhere, as well as the "*Adab, yā Hu*!" signs. The value and honor of Mankind is measured by how much *adab* he has. When you see the sign, "*Adab, yā Hu*!" be ashamed, O Man, and don't forget your Lord!

This is what *adab* is, the good manners. Who forgets his Lord has no *adab*; he is zero and he or she is ugly and no matter how much makeup they put on their face, they cannot be beautiful. The beauty that Allāh Almighty grants does not fade off a person's face, the beauty on the face of those who don't forget Allāh is the same until they go down to their graves. In the grave, when angels come they recognize them and their *nūr* and they question them accordingly. There is *nūr* on the faces of those who don't forget Allāh, there is joy in their hearts, there is happiness, and they succeed in every work they do! *Amān, yā Rabbī*!

Those who moved away from *adab* are all fighting each other; what they do is only to oppress, to kill, to burn, to destroy each other. May Allāh forgive us! Allāh did not create us to kill each other, but to be Believers. When we become Believers, the sword is lifted from us; otherwise, the Sword of *Qahhār* (Divine Wrath) comes and ruins the people. O our Lord! May You make us from those who always remember You, who never forget You!

How can you forget Who created you? Why don't you recite the *Bismillāh* and teach it? You put up portraits of political leaders and make people show respect to them, but you don't remember Allāh *Dhul Jalāl* and you don't recite the Bismillāh! Instead you put portraits, statues, idols, stones and plaques everywhere and you stand in front of them and worship them. This is a shame for the people! To forget The One Who created them is not suitable for Mankind! Man's honor is for his Lord Who granted him the honor and Who created him. May Allāh ﷻ make us from those who always remember their Lord!

Don't forget the *Bismillāh*; otherwise, you will have no value and everything you do will go wrong. Those who forget Allāh ﷻ always fight each other and Allāh Almighty says:

اذْكُرُونِي أَذْكُرْكُمْ وَاشْكُرُوا لِي وَلَا تَكْفُرُون

Remember Me, I will remember you. Give thanks to Me and do not be ungrateful towards Me.[79]

"Don't forget Me and I will not forget you! Some of them I feast with My blessings, I don't leave them, and some of them I leave forgotten. I forget those who forget Me; I don't forget, but I leave them as forgotten," because he doesn't accept The One Who created him nor remember His Holy Name.

They don't recite the *Bismillāh* even once and they never make *sajda*! Shame on them! We are not able to teach these things. They distort the minds of our children with all kinds of unnecessary, stupid, complicated things and drive them to Shayṭān's way. Shame on those people that don't make their children walk towards Allāh ﷻ! They don't teach the life that Allāh ﷻ accepts and they make their children to wander far away from it.

Remember Allāh and Rule Your Ego!

A person who forgets his Lord has no value left. Therefore, let us say, *"Bismillāhi 'r-Raḥmāni 'r-Raḥīm."* Don't forget, O my son! Don't forget Allāh Almighty or else you will be forgotten later. If you seek Allāh's help, say, *"Bismillāhi 'r-Raḥmāni 'r-Raḥīm"* and Allāh helps you in your every work. Some people say, "This one may help, that one may help," but it is not true. Say, "Allāh!" and He ﷻ sends you His honored, majestic servants who help you and inform you about His *Awlīyā,* and your every work becomes right.

Now they don't teach these things and the whole world has fallen into a state of madness. It is the year 2013 in their calendar. Today *dunyā* has fallen into its darkest era ever. Why? Because people are not saying, "Allāh." They make people forget Allāh and they whip the horse of Shayṭān! Shame on you, O People of the 21st century! Allāh knows how many centuries passed, but it is in the calculation of time that they know. O People of the 21st century! Collect yourselves, pull yourselves together and know the purpose of your life, know Who brought you into existence! Don't forget about His servanthood and you won't be forgotten, in *dunyā* as well as in *Akhirah.*

---

[79] Sūrat al-Baqara, 2:152.

Yā Rabbī! May You send us from Your servants who will teach us Your ways, send us Your sincere servants who will defeat Shayṭān. If they say "Be!" it will be and if they say, "Don't be!" it will not be, Allāh Almighty has such *Awlīyā*. If they say, "Stop!" it stops and if they say, "Carry on!" it carries on. They forgot the *Awlīyā* and they forgot the prophets. *Yā Hu*! This man has even forgotten Allāh! How can he ask about the Prophet ﷺ, how can he ask about the *Awlīyā*? The one they follow is Shayṭān.

Therefore, each country established a building without a foundation and now it has collapsed over their heads on the whole world, because what they built is a rotten building. In one quake all of them will collapse, the whole world! Unless Allāh Almighty keeps you, no matter what you build, it will collapse on your head, and the world has already collapsed, what they call 'the 21st century.'

Dunyā collapsed on the people of this century and they can't pull themselves out from under it. Of course you can't! What will pull you out is the Will of Allāh Almighty. When He ﷻ said, "Fall down!" the whole world fell down over these disobedient, denying and unbelieving people, and now they are trying to remove that debris. No you can't, because the debris is like a mountain and your power is like that of an ant. What turns the ant into an elephant is the power of Allāh ﷻ. What makes an elephant like an ant is again Him ﷻ. Step firmly! Step into the stirrup of the horse like a man and rule over your ego fully so that Allāh helps you! Allāh Almighty knows where you are going and knows that you are following Shayṭān, too, so He ﷻ leaves you and Shayṭān makes you ragged.

People Have Become Shaytan's Pets

Today Mankind is ridiculed by Shayṭān and has become the animal of Shayṭan. Come to yourself, O Mankind! Say, "I am man!" and don't do evil. All the people in the whole world learn evil and want to do it, and they sink themselves as well as others. O Lord, *tawbah, yā Rabbī! Tawbah, yā Rabbī! Tawbah, astaghfirullāh.*

Allāh Almighty says:

اذْكُرُونِي أَذْكُرْكُمْ وَاشْكُرُوا لِي وَلَا تَكْفُرُونِ

Remember Me and I will protect you with My mercies and remember you. Be grateful (make shukr) to Me and don't deny Me.[80]

What kind of man are you that you don't know what you do? Who doesn't know what he does is an animal. How can it be that a man doesn't know what he does? But your doings are like this. Before they used to say, "You do too much, but because all you do is evil, tie up your pants and then do it, it will come down between your legs! What is it that you are doing?" So this is what the whole world is doing and everyone keeps quiet, but this, my voice, will be heard in the east and in the west, because I have the intention to serve Allāh and am determined to destroy the Sulṭānate of Shayṭān, even in this old age of mine! Allāh ﷻ supports us and His Great Prophet ﷺ guides us! How beautiful is Islam! What a clean path Islam is! Every clean, pure act is in Islam and every dirty condition is in unbelief and in forgetting Allāh!

O our Lord! May You forgive us. I am weak, O Lord! I am weak, O Lord! *Qawwi dhaʿfi fi ridāq*. I am crying; I am crying to myself. I am sad and crying because of the troubles that those who misguided the people caused, loaded on the nations. I am sad and crying because of what Mankind is suffering through, but Mankind has fallen into such a state that they are welcoming what Shayṭān makes them do and they forget Allāh Almighty. *Amān, yā Rabbī! Tawba, yā Rabbī*! We ask *tawbah*, O Allāh, on their behalf also. *Tawbah, yā Rabbī!*

We started with *Bismillāhi 'r-Raḥmāni 'r-Raḥīm* and we finish with *Bismillāhi 'r-Raḥmāni 'r-Raḥīm*. May our grave be filled with *nūr* and may our destination be Paradise. O our Lord! May You forgive us. O Allāh! *Wa 'l-ḥamdulillāhi Rabbi 'l-ʿAlāmīn wa 'l-ʿaqibatu li 'l-muttaqīn, fa lā ʿudwāna illā ʿalā 'zh-zhālimīn. Yā Rabbī*! Don't make us from the oppressors nor leave us in the hands of oppressors!

It is *Rabīʿ al-Awwal*, the holy month of *Mawlid ash-Sharīf*, and it has been three days since it started. May our strength and joy be more! Allāh

---

[80] Sūrat al-Baqara, 2:152.

Almighty is with the True Ones, the *Sādiqīn*; Allāh Almighty is not with the those who are twisted. Twisted people are with Shayṭān. How do you tell if one is twisted? Because he is without the *Bismillāh*! The way of a person without the *Bismillāh* is twisted, it doesn't succeed, it is a dead-end road, it is dead. They will be finished, destroyed!

Yā Rabbī! Send us a *Ṣāhib* (Master), those who will teach us our religion, who will teach us our servanthood to You, who will make us keep the *adab* of our Prophet ﷺ.

Say, "*Yā Rabbī*! You are *Subḥān* (Glory)! You are *Sulṭān* (King)!" Say this and don't fear. *Yā Rabbī, tubnā wa raja'nā ilayk*! O my Lord! May You make our end a good end. *Yā Rabbī*! I am weak. Send us a *Ṣāhib* who will execute Your Order. You sent a sulṭān, but now *dunyā* is left without a sulṭān. Send us a sulṭān! Who is sulṭān? The one who starts with *Bismillāhi 'r-Raḥmāni 'r-Raḥīm* is Sulṭān. Those who worship portraits and statues become soldiers of Shayṭān in his way!.

Those who say "Allāh," are the soldiers of Allāh ﷻ and His Beloved ﷺ. May the Great Prophet ﷺ forgive us. He is *al-Shafi'* and *al-Mushaffa'* in the Divine Presence of Allāh Almighty; he ﷺ intercedes and his intercession is accepted.

Read the *Mawlid ash-Sharīf* in this holy month so that mercy rains on you; if not, they will suffer much more. May Allāh not make us from those who go astray as they are animals to Shayṭān.

Yā Rabbī! Forgive us and send us a Master. O Lord! Send us a sulṭān. *Tawbah, yā Rabbī! Tawbah, yā Rabbī, tawbah astaghfirullāh.* We repent for everyone and for ourselves also. We should say, "*Tawbah astaghfirullāh.*" We should say, "*Bismillāhi 'r-Raḥmāni 'r-Raḥīm.*" We should make *sajda,* even if it is two *raka'ats.*

Don't drink alcohol or troubles will come on your head. Don't smoke or you will catch a disease that can't be cured. Don't eat the dirty things or you will suffer troubles that can't be cured.

O our Lord! May You forgive us. O our Lord! Send us a sulṭān for the honor of Your Beloved ﷺ, may You send us one so that we see him and our children see him also. May our homes be joyous! May you recite the Holy Qur'ān in your homes, may *nūr* come and calamities go away from our homes, may *nūr* rain on us!

O People! Pull yourselves together or else this wheel of life will chop you up, finish you and throw you away. *Amān, yā Rabbī*! Forgive us. Send us a Master.

Wa min Allāhi 't-tawfīq. Fātiḥah.

Glossary

'abd (pl. *'ibād*): lit. slave; servant.
'AbdAllāh: Lit., "servant of God"
Abū Bakr aṣ-Ṣiddīq: the closest Companion of Prophet Muḥammad; the Prophet's father-in-law, who shared the *Hijrah* with him. After the Prophet's death, he was elected the first caliph (successor); known as one of the most saintly Companions.
Abū Yazīd/Bayāzīd Bistāmī: A great ninth century *walī* and a master of the Naqshbandī Golden Chain.
adab: good manners, proper etiquette.
Ākhirah: the Hereafter; afterlife.
al-: Arabic definite article, "the".
'alāmīn: world; universes.
Alḥamdūlillāh: praise be to God.
'Alī ibn Abī Ṭālib: first cousin of Prophet Muḥammad, married to his daughter Fāṭimah; the fourth caliph.
alif: first letter of Arabic alphabet.
'Alīm, al-: the Knower, a divine attribute
Allāh: proper name for God in Arabic.
Allāhu Akbar: God is Greater.
'amal: good deed (pl. *'amāl*).
astāghfirullāh: lit. "I seek Allāh's forgiveness."
Awlīyāullāh: Saints of Allāh (sing. *walī*).
āyah (pl. *ayāt*): a verse of the Holy Qur'ān.
dhikr: remembrance, mention of God in His Holy Names or phrases of glorification.
du'ā: supplication.
dunyā: world; worldly life.
Fātiḥah: Sūratu 'l-Fātiḥah; the opening chapter of the Qur'ān.
Grandshaykh: generally, a *walī* of great stature. In this text, refers to Mawlānā 'AbdAllāh ad-Dāghestānī (d. 1973), Mawlānā Shaykh Nazim's master.
Ḥadīth Qudsī: divine saying whose meaning directly reflects the meaning God intended but whose linguistic expression is not divine speech as in the Qur'ān.
ḥaḍr: present
Hajj: the sacred pilgrimage of Islam obligatory on every mature Muslim once in their life.
ḥalāl: permitted, lawful according to Islamic *Sharī'ah.*
ḥaqīqah, al-: reality of existence; ultimate truth.
ḥaqq: truth
Ḥaqq, al-: the Divine Reality, one of the 99 Divine Names.
ḥarām: forbidden, unlawful.
ḥasanāt: good deeds.
iḥsān: doing good, "It is to worship God as though you see Him; for if you are not seeing Him, He sees you."
imān: faith, belief.
imām: leader of congregational prayer; an advanced scholar followed by a large community.
insān: humanity; pupil of the eye.
Insānu 'l-kāmil, al-: the Perfect Man, *i.e.,* Prophet Muḥammad.
Jannah: Paradise.
jihād: to struggle in God's Path.
Jibrīl: Gabriel, Archangel of revelation.

Jinn: a species of living beings created from fire, invisible to most humans. Jinn can be Muslims or non-Muslims.
Jumu'ah: Friday congregational prayer, held in a large mosque.
Ka'bah: the first House of God, located in Mecca, Saudi Arabia to which pilgrimage is made and to which Muslims face in prayer.
kāfir: unbeliever.
lā ilāha illa-Llāh Muḥammadun Rasūlullāh: There is no deity except Allāh, Muḥammad is the Messenger of Allāh.
Madīnātu 'l-Munawwarah: the Illuminated city; city of Prophet Muḥammad; Madinah.
maqām: spiritual station; tomb of a prophet, messenger or saint.
ma'rifah: gnosis.
Māshā'Allāh: as Allāh Wills.
Mawlānā: lit. "Our master" or "our patron," referring to an esteemed person.
Miracles: of saints, known as *karamāt*; of prophets, known as *mu'jizāt* (lit., "That which renders powerless or helpless").
mi'rāj: the ascension of Prophet Muḥammad from Jerusalem to the Seven Heavens.
Muḥammadun rasūlu 'Llāh: Muḥammad is the Messenger of God.
mu'min: a believer.
munājāt: invocation to God in a very intimate form.
murīd: disciple; student; follower.
murshid: spiritual guide; *pir*.
mushāhadah: direct witnessing.
nabī: a prophet of God.
nāfs: lower self, ego.
nūr: light.
Nūr, an-: "The Source of Light"; a divine name.
raka'at: one full set of prescribed motions in prayer. Each prayer consists of a one or more *raka'ats*.
Ramaḍān: the ninth month of the Islamic calendar; month of fasting.
Rasūl: a messenger of God.
Rasūlullāh: the Messenger of God, Muḥammad ﷺ.
Ṣaḥābah (sing., *ṣaḥābī*): Companions of the Prophet; the first Muslims.
ṣaḥīḥ: authentic; term certifying validity of a *ḥadīth* of the Prophet.
ṣalāt: ritual prayer, one of the five obligatory pillars of Islam. Also, to invoke blessing on the Prophet.
ṣalawāt (sing. *ṣalāt*): invoking blessings and peace upon the Prophet.
salām: peace.
Salām, as-: "The Peaceful"; a divine name. *As-salāmu 'alaykum:* "Peace be upon you," the Islamic greeting.
Ṣamad, aṣ-: Self-Sufficient, upon whom creatures depend.
shahādah: lit. testimony; the testimony of Islamic faith: *lā ilāha illa 'l-Lāh wa Muḥammadun rasūlu 'l-Lāh,* "There is no god but Allāh, the One God, and Muḥammad is the Messenger of God."
eighth century *walī,* and the founder of the Naqshbandī Ṭarīqah.
shaykh: lit. "old Man," a religious guide, teacher; master of spiritual discipline.
shifā': cure.
shirk: polytheism, idolatry, ascribing partners to God
suḥbah: association: the assembly or discourse of a Shaykh.
SubḥānAllāh: glory be to God.

sulṭān/sulṭānah: ruler, monarch.
Sulṭān al-Awlīyā: lit., "King of the *Awlīyā*; the highest-ranking saint.
Sūnnah: Practices of Prophet Muḥammad in actions and words; what he did, said, recommended, or approved of in his Companions.
sūrah: a chapter of the Qur'ān; picture, image.
tafsīr: to explain, expound, explicate, or interpret; technical term for commentary or exegesis of the Holy Qur'ān.
tajallī (pl. *tajallīyāt*): theophanies, God's self-disclosures, Divine Self-manifestation.
ṭarīqat/ṭarīqah: lit., way, road or path. An Islamic order or path of discipline and devotion under a guide or shaykh; Sufism.
taṣbīḥ: recitation glorifying or praising God.
tawḥīd: unity; universal or primordial Islam, submission to God, as the sole Master of destiny and ultimate Reality.
'ulamā (sing. *'ālim*): scholars.
Ummah: faith community, nation.
'Umar ibn al-Khaṭṭāb: an eminent Companion of Prophet Muḥammad and second caliph of Islam.
'umrah: the minor pilgrimage to Mecca, performed at any time of the year.
'Uthmān ibn 'Affān: eminent Companion of the Prophet; his son-in-law and third caliph of Islam, renowned for compiling the Qur'ān.
walī (pl. *Awlīyā*): saint, or "he who assists"; guarḍian; protector.
zāwiyah: designated smaller place for worship other than a mosque; also *khāniqah*.
zīyāra: visitation to the grave of a prophet, a prophet's companion or a saint.

Other Publications (available at www.isn1.net)

Shaykh Muḥammad Nazim Adil

- New Day, New Provision (2014)
- Allāh Almighty Wants Us to Be Beautiful (2014)
- We Have Honored the Children of Adam (2013)
- Heavenly Counsel: from Darkness into Light (2013)
- In the Mystic Footsteps of Saints (eBooks) (2 volumes) (2013)
- Heavenly Showers (2012)
- The Sufilive Series (2010-12)
- Breaths from Beyond the Curtain
- In the Eye of the Needle
- Eternity: Inspirations from Heavenly Sources
- The Healing Power of Sufi Meditation
- In the Mystic Footsteps of Saints
- Liberating the Soul (6 volumes)

Shaykh Muḥammad Hisham Kabbani

- The Fiqh of Islam: A Contemporary Explanation of Principles of Worship
- *Al-Muṣliḥūn:* The Peacemakers, As Taught In Classical Islam (2014)
- Benefits of *Bismillāhi 'r-Raḥmāni 'r-Rahīm* & *Sūrat al-Fātiḥah* (2013)
- The Importance of Prophet Muḥammad in Our Daily Life (2013)
- The Hierarchy of Saints (2013)
- The Heavenly Power of Divine Obedience and Gratitude (2012)
- Salawāt of Tremendous Blessings (English/French/ Turkish/ Spanish)
- The Dome of Provisions (2012)
- The Prohibition of Domestic Violence in Islam (2011/Fatwa)
- The Sufilive Series (6 vol. 2010-12)
- Jihad: Principles of Leadership in War and Peace
- Cyprus Summer Series (2 vol.)
- The Nine-fold Ascent
- Who Are the Guides? (2008)
- Illuminations (2007)
- A Banquet for the Soul (2006)
- Symphony of Remembrance
- The Healing Power of Sufi Meditation
- In the Shadow of Saints
- Keys to the Divine Kingdom
- The Sufi Science of Self-Realization (also in French)
- Universe Rising: the Approach of Armageddon?
- Pearls and Coral
- Classical Islam and the Naqshbandī Sufi Tradition
- The Naqshbandī Sufi Way
- Links of Light: The Golden Chain
- Encyclopedia of Islamic Doctrine
- Angels Unveiled
- Encyclopedia of Muḥammad's Women Companions and the Traditions They Related

Hajjah Amina Adil

- Muḥammad: the Messenger of Islam (2001)
- The Light of Muḥammad
- Lore of Light / Links of Light
- My Little Lore of Light (3 volumes)

Hajjah Naziha Adil Kabbani

- Heavenly Foods (2011)
- Secrets of Heavenly Food (2009)

Lightning Source UK Ltd.
Milton Keynes UK
UKOW02f1804040914

238101UK00001B/4/P

9 781938 058264